TREASURE IN HEAVEN

Treasure in Heaven

The Biblical Teaching About Money, Finances, and Possessions

Virgil Vogt

Wipf and Stock Publishers
199 W 8th Ave, Suite 3
Eugene, OR 97401

Treasure in Heaven
The Biblical Teaching about Money, Finances, and Possessions
By Vogt, Virgil

ISBN 13: 978-1-55635-182-2
ISBN 10: 1-55635-182-8
Publication date 1/12/2007
Previously published by Servant Books, 1982

Contents

Introduction

I RECALL SITTING in our living room several years ago, talking to a middle-aged woman who had just handed me a check for $12,000. This constituted her entire life savings, her complete net worth. She was giving the money to Reba Place Fellowship as an open-ended, no-interest loan, with the distinct possibility that the principal itself might never be returned. The money was being offered to help us put together $15,000 which was needed for the down payment on an apartment building which we were trying to purchase.

The whole transaction was one of those unusual Kingdom of God events. We felt God leading us to undertake the purchase of this thirteen-unit building to meet the housing needs of a growing fellowship. However, the building, though conveniently located, was not on the market and we had no money. However, because we felt God leading us to do so, we began exploring the possibility of purchase. It turned out that the owner was willing to sell. And now, in an unsolicited and unexpected way, most of what we needed for the down payment was coming to us through this generous Christian woman. She was not a member of our church, but had heard of our need through one of the Fellowship members who worked in the same office. Little did he realize, when he shared with his office colleagues about our plans to buy the building, that one of his co-workers would become the principal source of financing!

However, the most striking part of what happened that day was not simply the unusual way in which the Lord met our needs, but the attitude of this gracious Christian woman. It was with joy, and a sense of relief, that she was transferring her entire life savings out of the bank and into the care of our Christian community. She had so thoroughly caught the

Kingdom vision that it made her a little nervous to have her money sitting around in the bank! For her, there was a distinct improvement in transferring the money to our Fellowship. I was moved by her sense that the funds would be more secure with us. And even though we were—and are—a tiny, struggling organization, I totally agreed with her. We laughed and rejoiced together; how wonderful and ridiculous it was! She left our living room that day, confident that her life savings were secure in the hands of God. Several years later, she wrote us saying that the loan would never be recalled. It had turned into a permanent gift!

Why this unusual approach to economics? This woman had caught a new approach to finances which is set forth in the teachings of Jesus. In his teachings and in his way of life, Jesus demonstrated a way of handling money which was refreshing, new, and breathtaking in its implications. When properly understood, his teachings are Good News in a world torn by injustice and weighed down with economic striving. Yet his ideas are so radical that they have been seriously neglected by the vast majority of Christians.

What a blessing it would be if the Christian churches of our time could more fully recover—and put into practice—the economic implications of the Gospel of Jesus Christ.

Our generation needs to hear Jesus on economics. Economic survival has always been a major life task for a great portion of the human family. And the temptation to become overly concerned with economic matters has been one of the basic spiritual pitfalls in every generation. Yet, never in the history of the world have these economic questions been thrust upon the human family with greater force than at the present time. Both the actual economic problems, as well as the overwhelming economic anxieties and temptations, are greater in our time than in any previous era of human history.

Never have so many been so prosperous. They live in mansions and eat the most exquisite foods from various parts of the earth. They enjoy unparalleled opportunities for travel, education, leisure, art, music, communication, political and economic activity. Large numbers of affluent elite are now found in nearly every country of the world. And in the countries of Western Europe, North America, Japan, and the oil-rich Arab states, the middle and upper-middle class people who participate in this luxurious way of life now number in the tens of millions.

In these affluent societies, the pressures to conform and participate are overwhelming. Attractive incentives have never been so numerous and so available, with something to elicit the devotion of every conceivable taste or ambition, be it noble or base. The pressure is on!

Yet, at the same time, never have so many been so destitute and poor! They are malnourished, ill-housed, often uneducated and unemployed. Frequently they are homeless, the victims of war and famine. Their political freedoms, even basic human rights, are easily trampled underfoot. These desperately poor number in millions, even billions. For them, economic questions are all-consuming—it is a matter of life and death. Their entire life energies are devoted to scraping together the barest necessities of life.

The physical and spiritual struggles inherent at each end of this economic spectrum, are compounded in our time by the extent to which they interact with each other. Through worldwide development of industrial society and multi-national corporations, the economy of the entire world is much more inter-dependent than ever before. Rich and poor compete for the same resources. And through the rapid development of world-wide communications, everyone is more aware than before of how the other half lives. This tends to intensify economic attitudes and motivations.

In addition, never has the instability of the economic order been more visible. The industrialized prosperity of urban civilization depends upon the successful functioning of an incredibly complex, worldwide network which is constantly being threatened by rising oil prices, skyrocketing interest rates, political upheavals, drought, labor unrest, rising expectations among the poor, emerging competitive systems, and many other similar developments. Millions around the world keep in daily touch with these struggles, following the most threatening features in their news media. Can you think of a more effective "setup" for keeping the men and women of the world anxiously devoted to their economic treadmills?

This whole complex of factors—practical, psychological, and spiritual—might best be pictured as a violent summer thunderstorm. We are living in a time of storms and floods. And as Jesus warned in his parable (Mt 7), many who look like they are doing well will suffer sudden destruction. The economic storms and floods of our time have done just that. They have destroyed long-established companies and driven many individuals and families to ruin. On a spiritual level, the impact has been devastating. Many Christian individuals and Christian grops have been intimidated or seduced into wholesale compliance with the economic evils of the day.

But there is a way to survive these stormy times: build on the rock. Jesus is the rock. Those who hear and obey the word of Jesus will stand and prosper in these tumultuous times.

ONE

Economics in the Old Testament

FROM THE VERY BEGINNING of his redemptive work, God has been teaching his people about how to approach possessions and finances. Although as with other areas, this revelation comes to unique fullness and clarity in the person of Jesus, it is useful to look at the Old Testament to see how God was preparing the way.

The Old Testament makes it clear that part of God's overall purpose for his people is abundance and prosperity. When God called Abraham to leave his country and kindred, he promised to bless him, and through Abraham to bless all peoples of the earth. "Now the Lord said to Abram. . . . 'I will make of you a great nation, and I will bless you, and make your name great, so that you will be a blessing. I will bless those who bless you, and him who curses you, I will curse; and by you all the families of the earth shall bless themselves' " (Gn 12:1-3).

In the book of Genesis, as well as throughout the Old Testament, it is obvious that this blessing included material abundance. The blessing promised Abraham was not just, or even primarily, economic—it was spiritual, personal, cultural, social, political—a comprehensive blessing which gave Abraham a unique place in the history of the world. But it definitely included material abundance. And the grandest part of the economic blessing promised to Abraham was God's gift of the whole land of Canaan. "Lift up your eyes, and look from the place where you are, northward and southward and eastward and westward; for all the land which you see I will give to you and to your descendants for ever" (Gn 13:14-15). God promised Canaan to Abraham and his descendants.

Yet just at this point of greatest economic blessing we see a surprising paradox. This man who was given the whole land did not possess a single acre of it for most of his life! Instead, "he sojourned in the land of promise, as in a foreign land, living in tents with Isaac and Jacob, heirs with him of the same promise" (Heb 11:9). Only at the time of Sarah's death did Abraham finally purchase and "own" a small portion of the land which was promised to him.

Abraham was prosperous in other respects. He had silver and gold, flocks and herds, family and servants in abundance. But in relationship to the land itself, we see a paradox which recurs elsewhere in God's dealings with his people. The Apostle Paul said it is like "having nothing and yet possessing everything" (2 Cor 6:10). God's overall purpose for Abraham was to receive the land, but God also chose to make this a matter of faith. Abraham was to trust God and move out on the strength of a promise. His security was to rest in the word of God.

The Exodus

We see a similar relationship between "having nothing and yet possessing everything" in God's dealing with his people at the time of Moses. God brought his people out of Egypt. He powerfully overcame Pharoah and the Egyptian army in order to deliver his people from slavery and oppression. Then at Sinai he revealed himself and his covenant and called the sons of Abraham to be his own people, a covenant nation to express his redemption.

Part of this redemption was economic abundance. God wanted to bring his people into a good and prosperous land, a land flowing with milk and honey. He wanted them to have cities which they did not build, vineyards which they did not plant. He wanted them to live in good houses, and he wanted their flocks and herds to multiply. God's plan included economic abundance along with all of the other blessings of being in a covenant relationship with the living God (Dt 8).

But it was also God's plan that his people should go through the wilderness before they got to the land of abundance. The amount of time they spent in the wilderness was greatly extended because of sin, but the wilderness experience itself was definitely part of God's plan in bringing his people into the land of abundance. Why? There were many important lessons to teach his people in the wilderness period, some of which were specifically economic. In fact, the wilderness is a great place for learning basic economics.

The arid and barren areas of the southwest United States give one a feeling for what it must have been like in the wilderness of Sinai. Scorching heat, rocks, scrubby thorn-filled plants, strange insects and desert reptiles, lack of water, absence of food—God's people had to camp out in a barren place like that for forty years. It was an excellent laboratory for Kingdom Economics 101.

Certain relationships can be more easily observed in a place of extreme poverty and deprivation such as the wilderness. In particular, God wanted the people to observe his relationship to the economic process. He wanted to strongly establish a few basic economic assumptions with them before allowing the people to enter their land of overflowing abundance.

The first lesson came quickly. The people were in the wilderness only a short time before they reached the point where just having the bread for each day and water to drink required a miracle of God. God supplied what the people needed because he wanted them to understand the nature of his involvement in the economic process. He wanted to teach them that their physical life and economic supply were gifts of his grace and that he was able and willing to supply what they needed, even when all normal sources seemed totally insufficient. God wanted them to know that he participates intimately in the economic process.

God's place in the economic cycle, so visible in the wilderness was equally necessary in the land of promise. It still required a miracle of God to put bread on the table and water in the well. The people still needed to depend on God, but his participation in the economic process was not so visible as it was in the wilderness.

We also see in the Exodus experience a sequential relationship between poverty and prosperity. Though God's ultimate goal was great abundance, the people needed first to go through a period of relative poverty in the wilderness. They had adequate provisions but their wilderness lifestyle was meager and austere. Yet the poverty of the desert and the abundance of Canaan were essential in God's plan for his people. Poverty preceeded abundance; each phase of the cycle gave meaning to the other. The experience of the wilderness cannot be understood unless it is seen as part of the journey into the land of abundance. Similarly, a proper understanding of life in the land of abundance requires remembering the time of poverty in the wilderness. "Take heed lest you forget the Lord your God . . . who fed you in the wilderness" (Dt 8:11-16). The full life of faith to which God called his people involved both phases—poverty and prosperity.

In addition to God's revelation of certain basic economic assumptions, he addressed the people directly about how they were to handle possessions and finances. It is significant that two of the Ten Commandments deal with possessions. Money has always been on the list of important topics God has addressed in redeeming his people. The Old Testament teachings on money and possessions fall into two broad streams. One deals with tithing; the other with economic justice. Many Christians are much more familiar with the tithing emphasis, but the justice tradition holds a key position in God's total revelation about finances and possessions.

Tithing: Feasting, Worship, and Care of the Poor

Tithing was related primarily to the worship life of Israel. Farmers were asked to bring one-tenth of all the produce of their lands and offer it as a sacrifice of thanksgiving and worship to God. Every tenth animal belonged to the Lord (Lv 27:32). Likewise, one-tenth of the grain, oil, and wine was set aside for the Lord (Dt 14:23). The produce thus designated had several specific uses within the life of God's people. On the one hand, this was God's way of making it possible for every ordinary Israelite to afford a week-long religious holiday, with feasting, at least three times a year! "And before the Lord your God, in the place which he will choose, to make his name dwell there, you shall eat the tithe of your grain, of your wine, and of your oil, and the firstlings of your herd and flock; that you may learn to fear the Lord your God always" (Dt 14:23). In short, tithes furnished the substance for the worship events and were utilized in sacrifice and feasting. By requiring each Israelite to set aside one-tenth of his produce for such nonproductive purposes, God built into the rhythm of life a continual reminder that he was the real owner of the land. It was only by his grace that the earth brought forth its abundance. The tithing system was thus a way of continually recalling the people to the lessons which God taught them in the wilderness.

A second use of tithes was to support the priests and Levites, who were set aside from most productive labor in order to carry out the teaching and worship life of the people. "To the Levites I have given every tithe in Israel for an inheritance, in return for their service which they serve, their service in the tent of meeting. . . . For the tithe of the people of Israel, which they present as an offering to the Lord, I have given to the Levites for an inheritance; therefore I have said of them that they shall have no inheritance among the people of Israel" (Nm 18:21, 24).

Finally, the tithes furnished income to support the poor, the fatherless, and the widows. "When you have finished paying all the tithe of your produce in the third year, which is the year of tithing, giving it to the Levite, the sojourner, the fatherless, and the widow, that they may eat within your towns and be filled, then you shall say before the Lord your God, 'I have removed the sacred portion out of my house' " (Dt 26:12-13).

Thus the Lord established the practice of tithing to keep each generation of Israelites in touch with the basic reality of God's involvement in the economic process. It enlivened the connection between everyday activity and worship, and furnished the resources for religious festivals, support of the priesthood, and almsgiving to the needy.

The proper care of the fatherless, the widow, and the poor in the land was an important concern throughout the history of Israel. Neglect and oppression of these needy ones was one of the basic sins for which Israel was sent into captivity (Am 2:6-7). The utilization of tithes for the support of such persons brings the tithing tradition into contact with the other set of Old Testament economic principles which directly address the economic relationships between various persons within the community of faith. This I call the "justice" tradition of Old Testament teachings.

Justice: God's Provision for the Poor

Both of the Ten Commandments which touch on economics are in the justice, not the tithing, tradition. The commandment against stealing forbids selfish grasping of the possessions of others. The commandment against coveting extends this prohibition into the realm of thought and desire. Even in the Old Testament, then, it is clear that a person's economic attitudes are as morally significant as his actions. This is an important revelation.

Many of the justice teachings are particularly concerned about the relationship between the rich and the poor. "He who is kind to the poor, lends to the Lord" (Prv 19:12). Also, "He who oppresses a poor man insults his Maker" (Prv 14:31). This word from the Wisdom literature recurs with clarity in both the law and the prophets:

> You shall not wrong a stranger or oppress him, for you were strangers in the land of Egypt. You shall not afflict any widow or orphan. If you do afflict them, and they cry out to me, I will surely hear their cry; and my wrath will burn.
>
> (Ex 22:21-23)

> Thus says the Lord of hosts, Render true judgments, show kindness and mercy each to his brother, do not oppress the widow, the fatherless, the sojourner, or the poor, and let none of you devise evil against his brother in your heart.
>
> (Zech 7:9-10)

The sojourner, the poor, the fatherless, and the widow were to receive special care. Remnants of grain were to be deliberately left in the field after the harvest so that the needy could glean them (Dt 24:19). They were to be specifically included in feasts and celebrations (Dt 16), and their rights were to be zealously guarded in administrative and legal decisions (Dt 24:17; Ex 23:6). This Old Testament attitude is well expressed in the Psalms: "Blessed is he who considers the poor! The Lord delivers him in the day of trouble" (Ps 41:1).

The justice tradition in the Old Testament included some important teachings about borrowing money. In the first place, if a poor brother asked you for a loan, you were required to give him what he asked. "You shall open your hand, and lend him sufficient for his need, whatever it may be" (Dt 15:8). Even the attitude in granting the loan is addressed. "You shall give to him freely, and your heart shall not be grudging when you given to him; because for this the Lord your God will bless you in all your work and in all that you undertake" (Dt 15:10). Furthermore, this loan was to made without interest. The prohibition against charging interest is clearly stated at a number of points in the Old Testament (Ex 22:25; Lv 25:36; Dt 23:19; Ps 15:5; Ez 18:8).

The significance of interest in the economic relationships between rich and poor is clear in the economic history of our own time. Charging interest helps create an economic system in which the rich benefit at the expense of the poor. It is true, of course, that the payment of interest is somewhat justified because the rich are making their resources available to the poor. In God's plan, however, the rich were to make their resources available *without* requiring this payment. The poor need these resources, yet they cannot really afford to pay the interest which is an additional burden in an already overwhelming situation. The net result is that the poor are continually paying a kind of tax that further enhances the position of the rich. The rich keep getting richer as some of the productive accumulation of the poor is continually channeled their way, and the poor often remain poor, or even get poorer.

The biblical pattern reverses this flow—God designed an economic system in which the rich were taxed to assist the poor. God's design is most dramatically expressed in a third Old Testament teaching concerning loans—every seventh year was a Year of Release, in which all debts were to be cancelled (Dt 15:2). Thus the accumulated surplus of the rich was not only available as a no-interest loan, but the Year of Release prevented permanent indebtedness. Every seven years, all of the poor in the land were to be given a fresh start, free of all debts. This, of course, cost the rich, forming an additional transfer of their surplus to benefit the poor. Significantly, the command to loan whatever your brother needs, whenever he asks, is given specifically in the context of this Year of Release. So even if your brother asked for help during the sixth year, you were required to loan him whatever he needed (Dt 15:9).

On the Year of Release, slaves were also to be set free. In biblical, as in modern times, there was a significant relationship between indebtedness and slavery. People became slaves in biblical times when they incurred great debts or sold themselves as indentured servants. In modern times, borrowing money creates a kind of partial bondage or slavery.

These three principles together—do not turn away a brother who is asking for a loan, give it without interest, cancel all remaining debts every seventh year—created a powerful thrust which substantially benefitted the poor, and yet did so in a way that avoided much of the paternalism and bureaucracy of the contemporary welfare system. It left the initiative and control very much in the hands of the poor man, along with his closest friends and neighbors. Those who were in a position to help did so actively, and in close contact with the people they were helping. The biblical pattern of assistance was offered without the binding quality of permanent indebtedness.

Putting these Old Testament teachings into practice today would represent a radical departure from our current practice. Yet, as we shall later see, the New Testament calls Christians to go even further.

Jubilee: Redistribution of Capital Wealth

Besides these provisions governing loans, the Old Covenant also contained a radical provision for redistributing capital. Once every fifty years, a Year of Jubilee was proclaimed. In addition to cancellation of loans and release of slaves, the land was returned to its original family ownership. In ancient times, the land was the primary capital resource of the community. There were a few other forms of wealth—silver and gold, flocks and herds—but the agricultural economy depended on the land. God's initial provision had been that the land be divided in roughly equal shares among all the families of Israel. Each was given a portion as their inheritance, decided by the casting of lots. The Jubilee Year was designed to redistribute the major capital resource once every fifty years.

God's plan for the Jubilee was obviously intended to help the poor and moderate the rich. He knew that some families would fall behind, while others would prosper exceptionally. The poor should not be permanently disinfranchised or penalized. In God's plan, they would get a fresh new start, of very substantial proportions, once every fifty years. To return the land to its original owners was a great gift to the poor but obviously painful and costly to the rich. For this reason, there were many periods in Israel's history when the Jubilee redistribution was not carried out. In fact, we have no definite records of its implementation. But it was clearly there in God's plan for his people.

Levites: Having Nothing But Possessing Everything

Another significant part of the economic revelation built into the experience of Israel were the Levites. All of the other tribes received a portion of the land as their inheritance, but the Levites did not. They stood in a different, once-removed relationship to the land. "The Levitical priests, that is, all the tribe of Levi, shall have no portion or inheritance with Israel; they shall eat the offerings by fire to the Lord, and his rightful dues. They shall have no inheritance among their brethren; the Lord is their inheritance, as he promised them (Dt 18:1-2).

Thus even after Israel entered the land of abundance, God wanted to preserve a portion of his people who would live without the normal means of economic productivity and depend upon him and the special provisions among the people of God for their sustenance.

The life situation of the Levites more closely paralleled the wilderness experience of obviously needing to depend upon God for daily bread, but it was a lifestyle to be lived out in a settled and prosperous land. The Levites "possessed everything"—they lived in a settled, prosperous land—but "had nothing" and depended on God for their daily bread.

Significantly, it was these people—called to renounce ordinary economic resources—who were to stand before God, worshiping him and ministering to the people. They had a unique theological and pastoral role within the larger community. And this correlated with having no possessions in the usual Old Testament sense. They were allowed to own homes and were also given cities. But they were cut off from the capital wealth and were dependent on God and the faithfulness of their fellow Israelites for the supply of their economic resources.

Economic Idolatry

By the time of the prophets—Isaiah, Jeremiah, and Amos, in particular—economic affluence in Israel was no longer a simple expression of the blessing of God; Israel's experience of prosperity had become a problem, even a sin. The prophet Amos denounced the wealthy Israelites of his time, "Woe to those who lie upon beds of ivory, and stretch themselves upon their couches, and eat lambs from the flock, and calves from the midst of the stall; who sing idle songs to the sound of the harp, and like David invent for themselves instruments of music; who drink wine in bowls, and anoint themselves with the finest oils, but are not grieved over the ruin of Joseph!" (Am 6:4-6).

These prosperous Israelites were so involved in business that even the sabbaths and religious festivals were an unwelcome interruption in the flow of economic development. Thus during the worship times, they would be thinking to themselves, "When will the new moon be over, that we may sell grain? And the sabbath, that we may offer wheat for sale" (Am 8:5). Their affluent life had been achieved at the expense of truth and justice. "They hate him who reproves in the gate, and they abhor him who speaks the truth. Therefore because you trample upon the poor and take from him exactions of wheat, you have built houses of hewn stone, but you shall not dwell in them; you have planted pleasant vineyards, but you shall not drink their wine. For I know how many are your transgressions, and how great are your sins—you who afflict the righteous, who take a bribe, and turn aside the needy in the gate" (Am 5:10-12).

And in their zeal for profits, their schemes and plans were not confined to the conduct of honest business but shaded over into fraudulent practices. "When will the new moon be over. . . . that we may make the ephah small and the shekel great, and deal deceitfully with false balances, that we may buy the poor for silver and the needy for a pair of sandals, and sell the refuse of the wheat?" (Am 8:5-6).

The desire for personal wealth had overruled concern for the poor and needy. Truth and justice were being perverted. Religious worship was insincere. And God was not impressed. "Therefore," God said through his prophet Amos, "they shall now be the first of those to go into exile, and the revelry of those who stretch themselves shall pass away" (6:7).

So we see that by this time in Israel's history, the temptations of affluence had corrupted the heart of God's people. This terrible disease was not confined to the rich businessmen of the time. Religious leaders had also become involved. The prophet Micah laments that Israel's "priests teach for hire, and its prophets divine for money" (3:11). Even the prophetic word had lost its integrity and was offered with a view to economic return. Micah describes the prophets as crying "'Peace' when they have something to eat, but declare war against him who puts nothing into their mouths" (Mi 3:5). The desire for prosperity had become the controlling influence in the hearts and minds of the people of God.

This economic idolatry was, in fact, one of the major sins of God's people at this time in their history. When the Lord addressed his people and through his prophets thundered out a call to repentance, one of its primary features was a return to economic justice. The integrity of Israel's worship could not be restored apart from a reordering of its economic life. Isaiah prophesied:

> What to me is the multitude of your sacrifices? says the Lord; I have had enough of burnt offerings of rams and the fat of fed beasts; I do not delight in the blood of bulls, or of lambs, or of he-goats. When you come to appear before me, who requires of you this trampling of my courts? Bring no more vain offerings; incense is an abomination to me. New moon and sabbath and the calling of assemblies—I cannot endure iniquity and solemn assembly. Your new moons and your appointed feasts my soul hates; they have become a burden to me, I am weary of bearing them. When you spread forth your hands, I will hide my eyes from you; even though you make many prayers, I will not listen; your hands are full of blood. Wash yourselves; make yourselves clean; remove the evil of your doings from before my eyes; cease to do evil, learn to do good; seek justice, correct oppression; defend the fatherless, plead for the widow. (Is 1:11-17)

Israel at this time was very religious. God's people conducted many solemn religious assemblies, brought many sacrifices and offerings, offered many prayers. But this religion God abhorred. He could not endure such religious celebration when the community was not attending to the needs of the fatherless and the widow, when economic justice was being neglected.

A similar word from God came through the prophet Amos: "I hate, I despise your feasts, and I take no delight in your solemn assemblies. . . . Take away from me the noise of your songs; to the melody of your harps I will not listen. But let justice roll down like waters, and righteousness like an ever-flowing stream" (Am 5:21, 23-24).

For those of us who live in a time of great economic injustice and economic idolatry, it is important to note how seriously God regards these issues. Dealing properly with economic matters is crucial to true biblical religion. "Is not this the fast that I choose: to loose the bonds of wickedness, to undo the thongs of the yoke, to let the oppressed go free, and to break every yoke? Is it not to share your bread with the hungry, and to bring the homeless poor into your house; when you see the naked, to cover him, and not to hide yourself from your own flesh? Then shall your light break forth like the dawn, and your healing shall spring up speedily; your righteousness shall go before you, the glory of the Lord shall be your rear guard. Then you shall call, and the Lord will answer; you shall cry, and he will say, Here I am" (Is 58:6-9).

God's word to Israel is clear. Whether in the form of rebuke and impending judgment, in the form of command, or in the form of promise, again and again God's word makes it clear that he is deeply concerned about the questions of economic justice. He wants the rich to take care of the rights and needs of widows, the poor, the fatherless, and the sojourner.

Yet even at this time, when economic idolatry had corrupted the hearts of God's people, God did not hesitate to describe the time of restoration which would come after the judgment as a time of great material abundance. Thus the prophets speak again and again of a time when the riches of the nations will pour into Jerusalem, when prosperity will be restored, when the hills will drip with sweet wine, and the plowman will overtake the reaper (Am 9; Is 60). Great prosperity was still a part of God's ultimate intention for his people, and he affirmed this at a moment in history when affluence had become the harlot that had led the people astray.

Covenant

Having briefly surveyed this Old Testament history it may be well to recall that in all the different stages of this story what God expected and what God did was taking place within the context of a covenant people. These principles were not addressed to scattered individuals, but to a gathered people, a people who shared a common destiny before the Lord. The economic principles were but a facet of this total reality. Without the other features of the covenant relationship the economic principles would not make sense. Nor would it have been possible to function as God suggested, apart from this covenant setting.

The covenant reality include God's gracious redemption as a free choice on his part. He chose and called Abraham. He intervened to deliver the people from Egypt. God's initial salvation was not contingent upon the good works of the Israelites. They, like we New Testament believers, were saved by a act of unmerited grace.

After bringing the people out of Egypt, God revealed himself to them in covenant. He identified himself as the saving God and set out commandments which were to govern their future relationship with him and with one another. They were to acknowledge him by obeying his commandments, and the basis for their obedience was his prior act of grace in saving them and choosing them for his own people. If they followed his commands, they would be blessed. If they did not, judgment and destruction would come upon them (Dt 28). The unusual economic teachings and the miraculous economic provisions were all instructions and developments which occured within the framework of this covenant.

The coming of Jesus as Messiah should be seen as arising from this Old Testament history. What is the revelation of God through his Son? What parts of the Old Testament are picked up and affirmed? What parts omitted or left behind? What new teachings does Jesus bring? In regard to economics, as in every other aspect, Jesus truly is the light of the world. God's revelation comes to fullness in him. And while there is much continuity between Jesus and the Old Testament, there is also much in him which is refreshingly new, going beyond anything that was conceived before his time.

TWO

Economics in the Message of Jesus

JESUS TALKED a lot about money and possessions. A new approach to property was an essential part of the Good News which he proclaimed. The economic message of Jesus is a truly astonishing one. Let us look at some of its main features.

Do Not Lay Up Treasures on Earth

Jesus taught that we should not lay up for ourselves treasures on earth (Mt 6:19), for "a man's life does not consist in the abundance of his possessions" (Lk 12:15).

These surprising words contradict the basic economic wisdom which has undergirded almost every society throughout the history of the world. Most of the world's people believe that you certainly should try to lay up for yourself treasures on earth because a man's life *does* seem to consist in the abundance of his possessions. The good life and material abundance appear to go hand in hand, so economic prosperity is highly honored throughout the world, and is sought with great devotion. But Jesus said, "Not so!" What rationale does he give for such an astounding proposal?

His initial point—surprisingly—is that it is a poor investment. "Do not lay up treasures on earth, where moth and rust consume and where thieves break in and steal, but lay up treasure in heaven, where neither moth nor rust consumes and where thieves do not break in and steal" (Mt 6:19-20). Jesus warns that earthly treasures are unstable and subject to loss. The forces of nature and the greed of other men conspire against us when we seek to accumulate wealth on earth. Decay and deterioration are built into the natural environment. They are inevitable. Greed and deception are equally pervasive among human beings. Those who seek for earthly wealth are bound to be defrauded and disappointed. And we often do see that those who have accumulated large fortunes are scrambling desperately to preserve and protect what they have collected.

Certainly the events of our own time demonstrate the instability of earthly riches. Inflation, one of the big current problems, is simply the cumulative effect of the greed of many individuals and groups. It makes some people rich quickly. But many who thought they were secure in their abundance now find it eroding away. Even vast and powerful corporations are the helpless victims of shifting economic forces. Who would have imagined in the 1950s that we would ever see Chrysler Corporation teetering on the brink of economic collapse? Many individuals who thought they had arranged for a comfortable retirement now find themselves struggling to survive. Treasures on earth, as Jesus said, are fundamentally unstable.

In making this point, Jesus appeals to our enlightened self-interest. Here, as elsewhere in his teaching, he presupposes that we are concerned about our own wellbeing. He doesn't ask us to set aside this self-interest, but rather suggests that we redirect our self-concern to a more secure and permanent solution. He doesn't want us to waste our energy and resources only to be disappointed in the end. So don't accumulate on earth!

A second reason Jesus gives for not laying up treasures on earth is that it affects the human spirit. "Where your treasure is, there will your heart be also" (Mt 6:21). We human beings have been created for something more lofty and worthwhile than simply groveling for our economic sustenance or even for economic affluence. To allow the human heart to be devoted to such mundane goals is to prostitute human creativity for ends that are totally unworthy of it. We are to be devoted to God and the Kingdom of God!

God created us in his own image—we were to be like him. When man corrupted himself and distorted this likeness, God intervened redemptively to restore us. Through Jesus we again have the potential of divine sonship. His own Spirit is within us! The whole Kingdom of God is our inheritance! We have been given a seat, not in the New York Stock Exchange, but in the courts of heaven (Eph 2:6), where the ultimate decisions of the universe are being transacted. Not only will we inherit the earth (Mt 5:5), but we are joint-heirs with Jesus Christ to all the riches of heaven as well (Rom 8:17), and in the coming ages, we shall govern the universe with him. In the present time, we are to be learning how to do this (1 Cor 6:1-6). For us to put our "heart" into earthly treasure is to repeat the folly of Esau, who sold his birthright inheritance for a single meal (Heb 12:16).

It is infinite tragedy and incredible waste for any human being—created for sonship in the courts of heaven—to be devoted heart and soul to a tiny fragment of earthly wealth. The whole thing belongs to us—why sell our souls for the privilege of controlling a mere pittance!

In our life at Reba Place Fellowship we have seen many individuals struggle with letting go of their earthly treasures. Traditionally one of the steps to membership in our community has been giving away all that you owned—either to the poor, to some other Christian cause, or to our own Christian community. Understandably, this is a big and difficult step for many people. Yet many individuals cling so desperately to so little. I've seen persons whose total net worth would not exceed $500 struggle desperately in not wanting to let go of their possessions. And in some cases, they couldn't let go, even of a few meager possessions, and were prevented from moving on to other things. God wanted to give them so much more, but they couldn't see it.

Isn't that a picture of the situation in which we all find ourselves! Even millionaires own a mere pittance, a meager $500 or so, in comparison to the Kingdom which God has prepared for us. Why cling to it?

The danger of accumulating possessions on earth is precisely that we will cling to them. We are easily enslaved by the things which we have carefully earned and saved, and our heart is readily drawn in their direction. This is a law of the universe, as sure as the law of gravity, and the greater the mass the more it pulls. Where your treasure is, there will your heart be also! If your treasure is on earth, your heart will be earthbound and mundane. If your treasure is in heaven, your heart can be participating in the life, power, and glory of God himself.

Many of Jesus' teachings consitute a warning against the dangers of wealth. He said it was hard, well-nigh impossible, for a rich man to enter the Kingdom. "How hard it is for those who have riches to enter the kingdom of God! For it is easier for a camel to go through the eye of a needle than for a rich man to enter the kingdom of God!" (Lk 18:24).

The story of the rich man and Lazarus (Lk 16:19-31) makes a similar point. The rich man when he dies goes to hell, while the poor man Lazarus goes to be with Abraham in heaven. When the rich man asked Lazarus to come and dip the end of his finger in water to cool his tongue and relieve his anguish, Abraham reminded him that in his earthly life he had received good things but Lazarus had received evil things. So now the tables are reversed and there is no way to change the situation.

In the parable of the great banquet (Lk 14:16-24), those invited offered various excuses for not attending—one wanted to inspect a recently purchased field, another wanted to test out his newly acquired yoke of oxen, and another was recently married. Work, property, and marriage—the good things of life in this world—can also be hazards that can keep people from the Kingdom of God.

Jesus knew how easily our devotion is turned to the wrong ends. And that is why he urged us not to accumulate treasures on earth, lest our heart become attracted to earthly properties and securities.

In summary, then, Jesus' rationale for urging us not to accumulate treasures on earth is grounded in two profound insights regarding human experience: 1) Earthly wealth is so subject to deterioration and loss that it represents a poor investment; 2) Seeking to lay up treasure on earth diverts the focus of the human heart from those Kingdom affections and directions which are more worthy of the sons and daughters of God.

Treasure in Heaven

If taken alone, the warnings and prohibitions of Jesus regarding finances sound fairly harsh. But in the teaching of Jesus, these are but a backdrop to his statement of a new approach. When we begin to glimpse what he advocates in a positive way, it is absolutely breathtaking! The things we are asked not to do become truly incidental when our vision beholds the opportunities which God has set before us. We are urged not to lay up treasures on earth, *so that we can "lay up for yourselves treasures in heaven"* (Mt 6:20). "The kingdom of heaven is like a treasure hidden in a field, which a man found and covered up; then in his joy he goes and sells all that he has and buys that field" (Mt 13:44). Once we see the value of the hidden treasure, we will sell whatever we must "with joy" because of the incredible investment opening up before us.

Unless we catch this positive vision, we will not understand Jesus in his approach to money and property. "Fear not, little flock, for it is your Father's good pleasure to give you the kingdom. Sell your possessions, and give alms; provide yourselves with purses that do not grow old, with a treasure in the heavens that does not fail, where no thief approaches and no moth destroys" (Lk 12:32-33).

The reality of God's gift of the Kingdom is the basis upon which we are called to "sell" and "give." Renouncing earthly treasures is simply the backdrop to acquiring heavenly ones. Here again we encounter the paradox between poverty and prosperity which appeared at several points in the Old Testament story. There, in fact, is a strong parallel between our present life experience and the wilderness period for Israel. We are going through a period of relative poverty, but are headed for a place of unfathomed blessing and abundance. The Kingdom of God in its fullness, which is yet to come, is not just a land flowing with milk and honey, but a place of unimaginable grandeur, peace, and joy. Pain, sorrow, and sin will have passed away. A new heaven and a new earth will be revealed, filled with the glory of God (Rv 21-22). It is because God has promised us the Kingdom, in all its glory, that we are called to sell our possessions, give alms, and lay up treasures in heaven. This is God's plan for us. Jesus is not asking us to give up the idea of abundance and quality of life. He is rather calling upon us to relocate the sphere in which we search for it.

Jesus' approach to laying up treasures in heaven is a novel one: "Sell all that you have and distribute to the poor, and you will have treasure in heaven" (Lk 18:22). "Sell your possessions, and give alms; provide yourselves with purses that do not grow old" (Lk 12:33). These statements do not imply that the heavenly riches of God must be painstakingly earned by our meritorious good deeds. The Kingdom is his gracious gift to us, completely out of proportion to anything we could earn. Yet within the context of this gracious gift, we are called to maximize our experience of it by purposefully focusing our own decisions in a way that connects with the Kingdom thrust. And in every poor person and every Christian brother or sister we find this opportunity to make a transfer of resources from earthly treasure to heavenly treasure.

Jesus invites us to look at human experience and the place of economics within it in a completely new way. This is well illustrated in the story of the dishonest steward in Luke 16, who was being fired from his position as Operations Manager because of inadequate performance. In the few hours or days which remained after he learned of his dismissal, but before he left the office, the dishonest steward created an alternative economic strategy. He called in his master's debtors one by one and wrote off twenty to fifty percent of what each one owed to his master, thinking to himself, "These people will receive me into their houses when I am put out of my stewardship."

If the dishonest steward had simply conducted business as

usual, on his final day in office, it would have gained him nothing at all. He was losing his position anyway. It was too late for business as usual, so he invented an alternate strategy which involved using economic resources for noneconomic goals. He used his master's money to make friends. And that is exactly what Jesus has in mind for us.

He commends the dishonest steward and invites us to develop a similar kind of alternative strategy for the use of money. "And I tell you, make friends for yourselves by means of unrighteous mammon, so that when it fails they may receive you into the eternal habitations" (Lk 16:9).

To simply manage our economic resources well, in terms of the normal understanding of good business management, is to misunderstand the meaning of this time in which we live and to miss the opportunity which God has set before us. We are also called to use economic resources for noneconomic purposes. We are told to "make friends" by means of "unrighteous mammon."

Our constant danger is that we will not see the opportunities which are set before us. In our accustomed way of looking at things we fail to comprehend all that is possible. We can live our lives in terms of the obvious, doing business as others do, giving and receiving according to the normal balance of human affairs. Or we can see beyond the present moment and go for stakes that are much higher. We can turn every mundane event into a Kingdom of God opportunity. "When you give a dinner or a banquet, do not invite your friends or your brothers or your kinsmen or rich neighbors, lest they invite you in return, and you be repaid. But when you give a feast, invite the poor, the maimed, the lame, the blind, and you will be blessed, because they cannot repay you. You will be repaid at the resurrection of the just" (Lk 14:12-14).

Notice the word "lest"! In Jesus' new approach it is *unfortunate* if things turn out as they usually do. If life returns to its normal ruts and our friends repay our invitation, then we have been repaid and our effort has no larger Kingdom significance. Only if the poor do not repay us does our dinner party become an incident of significance, part of the glory of Christ which shall be revealed in the church at the time of the resurrection! And it is not only the poor but our Christian brothers and sisters as well, who present us with these special moments of grace. With them we can translate our ordinary experience into the treasures of the Kingdom. For as Jesus said when he sent out his disciples to preach and heal, "He who receives you receives me, and he who receives me receives him who sent me. He who receives a prophet because he is a prophet shall receive a prophet's reward, and he who receives a righteous man because he is a righteous man will receive a righteous man's reward. And whoever gives to one of these little ones even a cup of cold water *because he is a disciple*, truly, I say to you, he shall not lose his reward" (Mt 10:40-42).

In the imagery of Revelation, the "righteous deeds of the saints" are what make up the "fine linen" of the heavenly wedding banquet (Rv 19:8). That is a good way to envision the purposeful impact of what we have accomplished within the total sphere of what God is doing. He is throwing the banquet and furnishing all that it requires. But our efforts now will make a difference then. Our presence at the banquet is a gift of grace, freely granted to all. Each of us is invited to make the banquet even more glorious by adorning and enriching what God has already established. We can enlarge and fill out the glory which will be manifested at the coming of Jesus Christ.

Time Is Short

Jesus frequently brought a strong eschatological view of human experience to his teaching about money. He wants us to see the end towards which we are moving. This is fundamental to his understanding of economics—"What does it profit a man if he gains the whole world and loses or forfeits himself" (Lk 9:25). "He who hates his life in this world will keep it for eternal life" (Jn 12:25).

The parable of the rich fool (Lk 12) is one of many which makes this basic point. Time is short, the end is near; these facts shape our approach to economic life. This parable might more appropriately be called "the parable of the successful businessman," since the man in the story did what most good businessmen would do. As his business expanded, he tore down his barns to build larger ones. And because of his unusual success, he planned an early retirement—soul, take your ease! From the normal business point of view, these are logical and appropriate decisions. But Jesus calls the man a fool—and he was! He had made no investment in the life which extends beyond death. All of his riches were in this world. He was not rich toward God. So at the point of death, he was completely impoverished.

Death is the irrefutable dividing line between this world and the age to come. If you haven't crossed that line voluntarily, by faith in Christ prior to death, you certainly will at the point of death. Jesus sets this eschatological fact before us as we think about economics.

Jesus usually brings this time factor into the picture by speaking about the reality of death and the contrast between this age and the age which is to come. He does not, in his economic teachings, emphasize the imminent end of the world. And it is well that he did not, for the end of the world has not come as quickly as many Christians thought. But death has and will come to us all—and rather quickly. This eschatological perspective pervades a number of Jesus' financial teachings and parables: the rich man and Lazarus, the parable of the wedding feast, the rich young ruler, the pearl of great price, the treasure hidden in a field, the parable of the last judgment, and many others. We cannot grasp or sustain the approach to economics revealed by Jesus unless we look at human experience from the perspective of eternity. Losing this perspective is one of our most constant errors.

In the parable of the dishonest steward, which we have already considered, it was the shortness of the time yet remaining for him in his position which led to the steward's novel strategy of using economic resources for noneconomic ends. Apart from such a foreshortening of the time, he would undoubtedly have conducted his master's business as usual. But with the end in view, he devised a new plan, which would carry benefits for him into the era beyond the termination of his job. Our relationship to time and to our possessions is similar. We have control only for a brief period. Within the framework of eternity, our seventy or eighty years on earth is but a whisper, a tiny speck on a vast horizon. Thus we need to approach our economic life in a way that will make sense in terms of eternity. The wisdom or folly of our economic stewardship will be most apparent at the moment of our death. We will know then whether we made most of our investments in this world, or whether we are "rich towards God" and have laid up much treasure in heaven.

"Stewardship" rather than "ownership" is the fundamental nature of our relationship to material possessions. The physical resources of this earth were here before us; they will remain after we depart. As Paul reminded Timothy, "We brought nothing into the world, and we cannot take anything out of the world" (1 Tm 6:7). The things which we control are not truly "our own." We are simply entrusted with them for a period of time. We are stewards who have been given responsibility to properly use some of the resources of the earth.

In every approach to economics, there is a tension between immediate gratification and long-term investment. Good management or stewardship involves striking a proper balance between these competing demands, giving to the present what is needed for the present, but diverting into long-range investment a significant part of the total resources. A steward or manager who spends too much on immediate needs and immediate gratification is always in trouble for the long haul. As sons and daughters of God, we have been allowed to look at the overall picture. We are invited to make investments that will be satisfying in the long run, to conduct our affairs in a way that will make sense in this life and in the age which is to come. This requires a certain balance. Some resources must be expended in meeting immediate needs. But wise stewardship involves channeling as much as possible into good, long-term, Kingdom of God investments, particularly since our control of present resources is limited to a very short time.

One of the couples in our church, like many in our time, are in a position where both husband and wife are employed full-time outside the home. But unlike many, they have determined that one salary is quite sufficient to sustain a modest, comfortable standard of living (this has more to do with their life-style than with the size of the salary). And they regularly contribute all of the second salary to the ministry of the church. Thus, their immediate needs are cared for adequately. But they are also investing for the future, like people starting a new business they are putting as much as they can into the Kingdom of God.

Another friend, after hearing some of this Good News at a weekend retreat, went home and with his wife, decided to redirect a significant portion of their monthly budget. Instead of putting the money into a fund for long-range retirement benefits, they decided to start giving it away each month. These people have caught the vision of investing in the Kingdom of God, and are finding great joy in doing so. As one of them said, "The Lord gave me faith to 'send on ahead' money I had previously been laying up on earth."

All These Will Be Yours As Well

After calling his disciples to radically surrender earthly securities and earthly treasures, Jesus repeatedly affirms that their daily needs will be cared for by their heavenly Father (Mt 6). In fact, considerably more space is given to these assurances than to the initial call—Jesus knew how much we would need the strength of these promises!

Of course God knows we need food and clothing, and if we seek first his kingdom and righteousness all these things shall be ours as well (Mt 6:33). Consider the rest of creation—the birds, the flowers. If God so wonderously cares for everything else, won't he much more care for us, his people, created in his image? "Oh men of little faith!" exclaims Jesus (Mt 6:30). Can't you understand the absolute reliability of the heavenly Father's provision for you?

Jesus assures us that we will receive the economic necessities of life, even when we have liberally disposed of the ordinary sources of such economic supply. "Do not be anxious, saying, 'What shall we eat?' or 'What shall we drink?' or 'What shall we wear?' For the Gentiles seek all these things; and your heavenly Father knows that you need them all. But seek first his kingdom and his righteousness, and all these things shall be yours as well" (Mt 6:31-33). To help us understand this, Jesus contrasts men of faith and the people of the world, "the Gentiles." He describes alternative approaches to the economic process, one characteristic of believers, the other of unbelievers. In the end, both groups are supplied with economic necessities. Those who seek the Kingdom *first* will also be supplied with necessities, but there is a great difference in the *way* they are supplied. The difference lies in what they seek. The nations of the world seek economic things—their desires, their imagination, their energies, plans, and systems of evaluation are all geared towards economic gain. But Jesus invites us to seek first his Kingdom. We are to invest the same kind of motivation, planning, and creative effort into building the Kingdom as the nations of the world put into economic development. There is a distinct contrast here in the object of our motivation and primary goal—so great, in fact, that Jesus said you cannot pursue both at once. "You cannot serve God and mammon" (Mt 6:24). These two approaches to the same reality are mutally exclusive; you are on one track or the other. He did not say that we simply should not, but that we cannot, serve God and mammon.

Jesus also contrasts the amount of responsibility which men of faith assume for economic provision and that assumed by the people of the world. The people of the world have to a great extent taken economic responsibility upon themselves. They work diligently at the economic task because they assume that everything depends on their own efforts. They think that they *must* provide for themselves. But Jesus calls us to acknowledge the limitations of our own efforts. "Which of you by being anxious can add a cubit to his span of life? If then you are not able to do as small a thing as that, why are you anxious about the rest?" (Lk 12:25-26). He calls us to recognize how little depends on us and how much we must, of course, be faithful in the little that is rightfully ours to do. We are expected to work and manage our resources well. But having done this, it is still clear that our finances are a gift from God, and that he assumes the greater responsibility for them.

Jesus makes a further point. Throughout this teaching, he sets forth anxiety as the characteric feature of a worldly approach to economic matters. Seeking to provide for yourself, and thinking you are able to, creates great anxiety! And well it should. We are over our heads when we try to play God's part. Instead, Jesus encourages his disciples to find a place of trust. Knowing God and allowing him to care for us brings us peace in a world characterized by great economic uncertainty and flux. If our security and provision were grounded in some part of the economic process, we would have much reason to fear. But our security and provision of daily necessities depends on the faithfulness of our heavenly Father, not on having money in the bank or possessing visible economic resources. That's the whole point of this teaching. We can be confident even when we have little or nothing, because our supply depends upon God and his faithfulness!

A great deal of the world's economic seeking and economic anxiety is focused on what will happen in the future. Jesus invites us to be free from these concerns. "Do not be anxious about tomorrow" (Mt 6:34). "Let the day's own trouble be sufficient for the day" (Mt 6:34). "Give us this day our daily bread" (Mt 6:11). We are free to take a rather short-range, day-to-day approach toward our economic provisions, while we take a long-term Kingdom of God view toward the total life process. We are free to divert resources into Kingdom investments because of the certainty of the fact that our own immediate needs will be supplied.

With all of these strong assurances of how God will provide

for the needs of his people, is it conceivable that a good Christian might starve? Of course. There are times when God chooses to allow us to suffer along with the rest of mankind. Sometimes Christians suffer when widespread destruction comes upon the world, and at other times we suffer through persecution that arises on account of our faith. Yet in all of these circumstances we can proceed with the confidence expressed by Daniel's three friends when they went into the fiery furnace! "Our God whom we serve is able to deliver us from the burning fiery furnace; and he will deliver us out of your hand, O king. But if not, be it known to you, O king, that we will not serve your gods or worship the golden image which you have set up" (Dn 3:17).

Our confident knowledge of God's willingness to provide for us, and his commitment to do so, gives us the assurance that any interruption in this supply, be it temporary or permanent, is not an accident or something happening apart from his awareness and permission. If not even a sparrow falls to the ground without the Father's will (Mt 10:29), as Jesus confidently asserts, we can be sure that we will not starve to death without the Father's will. And if he wills it, we have nothing to fear.

Jesus was without food for forty days in the wilderness. Paul spoke of "toil and hardship, through many a sleepless night, in hunger and thirst, often without food, in cold and exposure" (2 Cor 11:27). Both Jesus and Paul experienced severe deprivation in their physical existence, but this did not represent a failure of the Father's love and care. In fact, the very occasion of these deprivations allowed him to reveal his care and provision. Paul wrote elsewhere, "We have this treasure in earthen vessels, to show that the transcendent power belongs to God and not to us. We are afflicted in every way, but not crushed; perplexed but not driven to despair; persecuted, but not forsaken; struck down, but not destroyed; always carrying in the body the death of Jesus, so that the life of Jesus may also be manifested in our bodies" (2 Cor 4:7-10).

The life of discipleship involves suffering. It involves affliction, persecution, being struck down. When Jesus spoke of the "hundredfold" provision of the Father, even in this life, he carefully added, "with persecutions" (Mk 10:30). The sufferings we experience become the occasion for manifestation of the power of the resurrected Lord. Certainly our knowledge of the Father's love and care should not lead us to picture life as comfortable and safely intact, but rather, it should lead us to see our sufferings as purposeful (1 Pt 1:7) and temporary. "And after you have suffered a little while, the God of all grace, who has called you to his eternal glory in Christ, will himself restore, establish, and strengthen you" (1 Pt 5:10). The important point, for this discussion, is that the presence of these sufferings does not diminish our certainty of the Father's daily care and provision for each one of his children.

A lack of confidence regarding the supply of our own needs is one of the greatest deterrents to really following the teachings of Jesus regarding money. But the history of the church is full of wonderful stories regarding the way God has fulfilled his promise to provide for us.

I recall an incident in my own life when as a young man I was just learning to trust God to supply my needs. Before coming to Reba Place Fellowship, I was the pastor of a church near Ft. Wayne, Indiana. We often operated on a very limited personal budget, which was good for learning basic lessons in trusting God. At one point I accepted an invitation to visit a small church in Iowa and conduct a week of meetings. But as the time for going to Iowa drew near, we were completely out of money.

This was not unusual in those days, and I simply laid the matter before the Lord and looked to him for the money. In this situation, as in others, I thought, if I am doing what he wants, I can expect him to provide the necessary resources. However, as days went by and no money appeared, deciding what to do became increasingly difficult. I considered borrowing money to make the trip, but that did not seem consistent with what the Lord had been teaching us. So I finally put it to the Lord in this way: "Lord, if you want me to go, you have to supply the money. If I don't get the money, I'm not going. Perhaps I misunderstood your direction in accepting the invitation. In any case, if I don't have the money to go, I'll call the pastor in Iowa and tell him I am unable to come." This was a satisfying resolution, although to realistically open myself to the possibility of cancelling the meetings at the last minute was difficult. Still, it seemed right to work out the problem in this manner between myself and the Lord.

I had train reservations for early Thursday morning. On Wednesday evening, we were still without money. I decided to wait until Thursday morning to see the final outcome. If I still had no money, then I would make the call.

We went to a prayer meeting at the church that evening, and after the meeting, two people came up and slipped me a few dollars as we were exchanging greetings. It never happened before, or since, that any one handed me money after a Wednesday evening meeting. But on this particular evening, two people did! And between them they contributed enough money to pay for the train tickets, with a little left over for my wife, Joan, to use in my absence. When I boarded the train early the next morning, I was confident that God himself wanted me to conduct that set of meetings! It was a joyful experience to know that I was doing what he wanted and that he was providing the resources.

The meetings were blessed by the Lord. During the course of the week I preached about the teachings of Jesus in regard to money, and the scripture that the Lord set before me was Luke 21:1-4, the story of the widow who put her whole living into the offering. I wanted to lift up the example of this woman, as Jesus had done, to illustrate the principles of Kingdom economics. He said that she, out of her poverty, put in more than all of the rich who gave out of their abundance. But as I prepared for this meeting, the Lord convicted me personally. Was I really willing to put my whole living into the offering? Earlier in my life, I had sought to renounce all for the sake of Christ. But what about now? As I continued to pray over this matter, it became increasingly clear that I could not preach a message on that text unless I was sincerely willing to do exactly what the widow had done. As I waited upon God, I not only felt myself become willing, but joyfully willing to do so. And I decided that when I returned home, my next paycheck would be given entirely. I would simply endorse the check and put the entire amount into the Sunday morning offering. This was a difficult decision, since we needed the money for living expenses. But it seemed like the right thing to do because God was leading me to do it. I did not know how we would make up for the loss of income. But I had confidence that God would supply our need, and I enjoyed preaching on Luke 21 that evening!

At the end of the week, the church decided to take up an offering to cover my expenses. Since it was a small church, I didn't expect much. In fact, I had assumed all along that if my travel expenses were repaid, and perhaps a small honorarium in addition, I would be doing well. However, the church gave generously. And what brought particular joy to my heart was the fact that after travel expenses had been paid, the amount remaining was almost exactly what my next paycheck would be—the one I had decided to put into the offering. So even before I had an opportunity to carry out my commitment to the Lord, he graciously and faithfully provided for the needs of my family.

We have had many other experiences of this sort over the years. In our life at Reba Place Fellowship, we have often operated on a rather tight budget, yet opportunities for ministry keep coming, ministries that cost a lot of money. New people come who need help, situations arise that require additional staff time. As we prayerfully move forward in faith, seeking God's Kingdom but not knowing where the money will come from, God faithfully provides for all of our needs. It was undoubtedly out of many experiences of this sort that Paul could confidently exclaim, "God is able to provide you with every blessing in abundance, so that you may always have enough of everything in abundance for every good work" (2 Cor 9:8).

As we seek first the Kingdom of God, all these things will certainly be ours as well.

Renunciation At the Beginning

In Luke 14, Jesus reviews the basic call to discipleship. He begins by saying that unless we hate our own father, mother, wife, children—even our own lives—we cannot be his disciples. "Whoever does not bear his own cross and come after me, cannot be my disciple" (Lk 14:27). He then ends this section by saying, "Whoever of you does not renounce all that he has cannot be my disciple" (Lk 14:33).

Jesus is talking here about the most fundamental relationships of human life—family, our sense of self, and our relationship to our possessions. This is the basic stuff out of which personal identity and experience is fashioned. Yet Jesus says that we must renounce it all. A "cross" experience must come between us and these most dearly loved and most necessary things. These are not evil, sinful things—they are the good and beautiful things of life. We are called upon to voluntarily surrender the sustaining sources of our existence. Paul was certainly speaking of this very thing when he wrote to the Galatians and said, "Far be it from me to glory except in the cross of our Lord Jesus Christ, by which the world has been crucified to me, and I to the world" (Gal 6:14).

The person who has experienced this profound realignment of inner-life connections has a totally new approach to human experience. Paul said of himself, "I have been crucified with Christ; it is no longer I who live, but Christ who lives in me; and the life I now live in the flesh I live by faith in the Son of God, who loved me and gave himself for me" (Gal 2:26). Jesus presents the call for this "cross" experience—this renouncing of all—not as the end goal of mature faith, but as a prerequisite for discipleship. Unless you do these things, he said, you cannot be my disciple. This is the starting point for discipleship—complete renunciation, an inner letting go of our need for and dependency upon all these "necessary" things.

In putting it this way, Jesus offers a fundamental insight into spiritual growth and formation. Renunciation of all things is what he seeks at the foundation of our Christian experience.

This includes renouncing our possessive approach to material belongings. As people come to the Lord and become established in the faith, a wholehearted economic renunciation should be a normal part of the experience. Failure to deal realistically with economic issues at the beginning of one's Christian life makes believers vulnerable to confusion and compromise as they go on in their walk with the Lord.

For some persons this renunciation will take the form of actually selling everything and giving it away. This was the advice Jesus gave the rich young ruler: "One thing you still lack. Sell all that you have and distribute to the poor, and you will have treasure in heaven; and come, follow me" (Lk 18:22). People often suggest that this was a special word to a young man who had a particular problem with materialism—and he obviously did have a problem. He was so attached to his possessions that he was unable to accept the invitation of Jesus. But Jesus gave a similar invitation, in the form of a general call, which seems to be addressed to all of his disciples: "Fear not, little flock, for it is your Father's good pleasure to give you the kingdom. Sell your possessions, and give alms; provide yourselves with purses that do not grow old, with a treasure in the heavens that does not fail, where no thief approaches and no moth destroys" (Lk 12:32-33).

In our time we need to strongly affirm that renouncing our possessions by actually selling them and giving it all away is a good and reasonable way to start out as a disciple. This has become such a rare occurrence in normal Christian experience that it needs particular emphasis. The invitation of Jesus, "Fear not, little flock," still stands.

It is also clear from the Gospels that selling all and giving it away is not the only way for this renunciation to occur. Zaccheus, for example, only gave away "half" of his goods, plus, of course, restoring fourfold to all who had been defrauded. Yet this was the spiritual equivalent, for he had caught the vision and was responding wholeheartedly. Jesus confirms this as he exclaims, "Today salvation has come to this house" (Lk 19:9).

If we look at just these examples, we could already conclude that some disciples give away all that they have, and others only give away half. Yet both of these actions may represent the same spiritual reality. Of course, giving away half would not represent the same spiritual reality if it was undertaken for the purpose of avoiding the need to give it all away! But if the inward willingness to give it all away is really there, the practical expression of this doesn't make much difference. I have known people who were ready to give it all away, but had very little opportunity to give away anything. For example, a woman whose husband is not a Christian may have very little separate control of family finances and therefore no opportunity to give it all away.

When inward renunciation is not accompanied by an outward dispersal of resources, we still need to find ways to express and experience it. I was once trying to help someone work through this process of total renunciation for the sake of following Christ. After we had talked about it at length and experienced the spiritual reality of renunciation, I got out a blank sheet of paper and asked the person to sign at the bottom. This was done with the understanding that God would fill in anything he wanted on the blank page. It was like signing a blank check and giving it to God. The details of what God actually wanted would emerge later, but the person's total agreement to do whatever the Lord required was offered at the beginning. It was a moving experience, made real by the Spirit of God in the heart of my friend. In the years that followed, the content, unknown when my friend signed the "check," emerged with clarity. There were big and costly steps as God filled in the blanks. It eventually involved much selling and giving, as well as leaving home and friends for the sake of the Gospel. But the signature, and the renunciation which it represented, were genuine, and each time God's will became clear, it was met with a definite yes.

In Timothy 6 Paul provides an interesting glimpse into the way this was worked out in the early church. On the one hand, it is clear in his counsel to Timothy that some of the believers still possessed much wealth. They did not sell all and give it away at the beginning of their Christian lives. Paul writes, "As for the rich in this world, charge them not to be haughty" (2 Tm 6:17). It is obvious from the instructions that follow that Paul is referring to rich believers. So some of the brethren still had many possessions at their disposal. On the other hand, what Paul recommends for these rich believers boldly envisions that they will now be carrying out the key concepts of Kingdom economics as taught by Jesus. He says, "Charge them not to be haughty, nor to set their hopes on uncertain riches but on God who richly furnishes us with everything to enjoy. They are to do good, to be rich in good deeds, liberal and generous, thus laying up for themselves a good foundation for the future, so that they may take hold of the life which is life indeed" (1 Tm 6:17-19).

Notice how he recalls primary themes in the teaching of Jesus: do not set your hopes on earthly riches because they are uncertain; put your confidence in God who richly furnishes us with everything; do good, be rich in good deeds, liberal, generous, i.e., give, give, give; by so doing you will lay up treasures in heaven! So believers who have abundant possessions are invited to become part of God's open-ended Jubilee which brings good news to the poor. Certainly an inner renunciation would be a necessary prerequisite for participating in such a bold Kingdom approach to finances.

Renunciation and the Powers

The renunciation Jesus calls for can greatly free us from spiritual powers that control life in the world. Significantly, Jesus put the discussion of economics into the realm of spiritual powers by using the concept of "mammon" (Mt 6:24). This way of speaking about money gives it a personal and spiritual character. The word which Jesus uses at this point in his teaching is apparently an ordinary Aramaic word for money or wealth. But scholars have been unable to find any other use of the term which personifies mammon as a kind of god. None of the religions of the time had a god by this name. So the concept itself seems to be original with Jesus. By putting it this way, he is trying to make it clear that in dealing with money, there is much more at stake than a simple medium of exchange. Money is not something morally neutral, a resource for good or ill, depending entirely upon our own attitude toward it. In the realm of economics we are dealing with a power outside of ourselves which tends in the wrong direction. Jesus uses this same concept again in Luke 16, with unmistakable clarity, when he describes ordinary riches with the term "unrighteous mammon" (Lk 16:9).

We need to understand finances in the context of principalities and powers. The biblical view of the world is that God's creation includes "visible" and "invisible" realities (Col 1:16). The invisible reality, which was originally a part of God's "good" creation, is variously described to include such things as thrones, dominions, principalities, and authorities (Col 1:16). Various political and social systems which we can see have a spiritual or invisible background which we cannot see. The biblical writers seem to suggest that governments and other similar authorities in the world are energized and controlled by spiritual forces which have a certain order and position within the total creation. Before coming to Christ, we were all under the control of these "elemental spirits" (Gal 4:8-11; Eph 2:1-5).

The "powers," once a good part of God's creation and intended by him to sustain and order various aspects of life in the world, have now—because of sin—lost their proper position. They continue to function, often very effectively, but without a proper orientation toward God as the center of all things. That is why these "powers" bring us such mixed results. On the one hand, they bless us and bring many good things into our lives. But as we enter into the process and become part of the world system or world approach, we often find ourselves drawn away from God. We find depersonalization and destruction built into the very fabric of the world system.

Mammon is one of these powers. Many good things come to us out of the economic process. Work, property, agriculture, commerce—what man has developed in these areas over the years is phenomenal. The ability to support life and enrich life which flows from the business systems of the world certainly reflect the creativity established by God. And yet there is something fundamentally wrong. Many people get hurt. Some are well provided for and others deprived. Work is mismanaged, people corrupted, the earth is polluted, and man is drawn away from God. The thing that ties us into this world system and puts us under the control of spiritual "powers" is the notion that certain things belong to us and that our survival is linked to maintaining these possessions or securing benefits which the world provides. We will do whatever the world asks to maintain these benefits if we think that our survival requires it. We will not risk violating the system or the "powers." Jesus calls for an inward renunciation—a letting go of all that we have—right at the beginning of our Christian experience—so that we will not be manipulated by the economic circumstances around us. We are to be free to follow God and walk in newness of life.

It may be useful here to observe that much of the teaching of Jesus about economics is actually evangelistic in character. Many of his parables and teachings are not primarily instructions to his disciples about how they should live, but proclamations of the Good News. They are designed to help people make the initial jump by seeing the folly of the world's system, the wisdom of investing in the Pearl of Great Price.

Receiving a Hundredfold

God's economic plans are full of surprises. First, he tells us to give up everything we have, to renounce it all. Logically, then, considering this command and all the warnings Jesus gives about the dangers of riches it would seem that we are headed for a very barren life-style, devoid of material resources except for the barest of necessities. But, as it turns out, that is not God's intention. What he has in mind for us is something more complex and more wonderful.

The surprising nature of his intention comes through in an encounter with the disciples which is recorded in Mark 10. The situation—which has been referred to earlier—gets underway as Jesus articulates the call of total renunciation to a rich young ruler who is seeking his advice. Jesus says to him, "You lack one thing; go, sell what you have" (Mk 10:21). Upon hearing this, "his countenance fell, and he went away sorrowful; for he had great possessions (v. 22). Mark continues:

> Jesus looked around and said to his disciples, "How hard it will be for those who have riches to enter the kingdom of God!" And the disciples were amazed at his words. But Jesus said to them again, "Children, how hard it is to enter the kingdom of God. It is easier for a camel to go through the eye of a needle than for a rich man to enter the kingdom of God." And they were exceedingly astonished, and said to him, "Then who can be saved?" Jesus looked at them and said, "With men it is impossible, but not with God; for all things are possible with God" (vv. 23-27).

This incident profoundly reaffirms the radical evangelistic call of the Kingdom of God, which includes renouncing all to follow Jesus. Peter then reflects on their own experience, "Lo, we have left everything and followed you" (v. 28).

Here comes the surprise. It doesn't seem to follow logically from what has just been said. But Jesus says, "Truly, I say to you, there is no one who has left house or brothers or sisters or mother or father or children or lands, for my sake and for the gospel, who will not receive a hundredfold now in this time, houses and brothers and sisters and mothers and children and lands, with persecutions, and in the age to come eternal life" (v. 29-30).

This is an important scripture, for in it we have one of the clearest and most revealing statements of Jesus regarding the life-style which he envisions for those who hear the evangelistic call and renounce everything to follow him. There can be no question here but that these two belong together—the invitation to sell all, and the promise of lands and relationships a hundredfold. Had this word occurred in any other context, we would probably conclude that he had two different sets of people in mind—those called to renounce everything and live an ascetic life without material benefits, and those called to have many houses and lands. But this kind of logical distinction is precluded by the clarity of the situation. The renunciation of all things and houses a hundredfold belong together in the experience of Jesus' disciples.

How can we understand this? First, let us note a sequential relationship. It is somewhat like the wilderness and the promised land of the Old Testament. Those who are invited to follow Jesus are first of all called to renounce all that they have, in some cases even to sell it and give it away. Receiving a hundredfold houses and lands is a promise to those who have taken the first step. They don't happen at the same time. The step of renunciation must preceed the step of receiving God's gracious multiplication of all that we have given up.

It may help to recall that the message of Jesus concerned the Kingdom of God. He was inviting men and women to enter the Kingdom, to seek first the Kingdom. The hundredfold brothers and sisters, houses and lands simply reflects the reality of this Kingdom. While it is yet to be revealed in its fullness, to some extent we live in this Kingdom reality now. As sons and daughters of God we have already passed from death to life. And it is among those who believe and follow Jesus that the Kingdom is manifested. Within this covenant circle there are a whole new set of relationships. Other believers become our brothers and sisters, and our lives are linked with them in a most profound way. Their houses become ours and our houses theirs. Thus through the love and sharing of believers, we experience the reality of this promise—we have houses and lands a hundredfold. As sons and daughters of the Kingdom we have access to all the resources of Kingdom's citizens.

The life-style to which we are called, as we renounce all to follow Jesus, is not a barren and impoverished life-style in which we squeak by with a few relationships and hardly any possessions. Instead, we are invited to experience a miraculous richness of life, with more relationships and more houses and lands at our disposal than would have been possible under any other circumstances. Unfortunately, many Christians still cling cautiously to the few relationships and possessions which they brought with them into the Kingdom and are not able to see or receive the abundance which God has prepared. Nor do they contribute much towards helping other believers experience the hundredfold blessing of God.

However, this promise of material abundance seems to present a problem. Doesn't all this abundance merely repeat the situation that we were trying to avoid? People of the world are seeking material abundance and we thought Jesus was calling upon us to give it up. Now what is all this? Aren't we back in the same situation we started in? Won't the hundredfold houses and lands prove to be a spiritual problem for Christians. Perhaps. But not necessarily. If we can learn and maintain the things which God has revealed about finances, the two situations will not be the same. They are so different, in fact, that Jesus said we cannot be in both at the same time. It's either God or mammon. If we take the way outlined by Jesus and stick with it, we will be involved in economic realities and will even be involved with houses and lands in great number, but it will still be different.

For instance, how we get this abundance is different. The hundredfold houses and lands spoken of by Jesus are received as a gift from God given to those who are not seeking houses and lands. They are seeking the Kingdom. Furthermore, the abundance of the Kingdom is maintained without our clinging to it or trying to protect it. In fact, we are taught to be very free with our possessions, to give them and share them. The hundredfold abundance exists precisely because there is so much sharing. And what these possessions mean to us is different. Our renunciation doesn't stop with the initial step. Paul expresses this in Philippians when he says, "Whatever gain I had, I counted as loss for the sake of Christ" (3:7). This is past tense and describes our renunciation at the start of our discipleship. But then he continues in the present tense, "Indeed, I count everything as loss because of the surpassing worth of knowing Christ Jesus my Lord" (v. 8). When this is the attitude of our hearts, we can honestly say that the things we possess are not our own. We can live in the world and utilize houses and lands without diminishing our relationship to God.

Jesus tried to share this important lesson with his friends, Mary and Martha. "Martha, Martha, you are anxious and troubled about many things; *one thing is needful.* Mary has chosen the good portion, which shall not be taken away from her" (Lk 10:41-42). Those who have learned to seek the one needful thing, to count all things as loss for the sake of knowing Christ, are free to receive the manifold gifts of God without developing an illicit dependency on the gifts rather than remaining wholeheartedly in love with the Giver.

Jesus promises that God will give generously to all who have left everything for him (Mk 10). He will not only furnish them with food and clothing, as indicated in Matthew 6, but with brothers and sisters, houses and lands a hundredfold—all in this age—and in the age to come, eternal life!

The financial questionnaires I have filled out are often humorous. I don't own a house or a car. I don't own a business or a farm. I don't have any savings or any debts. And between Joan and myself our cash assets may range anywhere from $100 to $300. It looks pretty thin.

And yet, I do have a place to live, we can usually find a car to drive when we need one, and there are hundreds of homes throughout this country and around the world which are completely at my disposal. I can walk into any one of them at any time and make myself completely at home, just as though I owned the place—for in a sense I do, although someone else lives there all the time and the legal title is in their name. But I am welcomed as warmly as though part of the family, and I am.

There are homes in the inner city, humble but full of warm Christian love. There are fancy suburban mansions with all the latest gadgets. I find brothers and sisters almost everywhere I go. They welcome me like a member of the family. They drive me around. They fix their finest meals for me. They give up their beds so I can stay overnight. They pray for me when I am sick. They share with me the deepest yearnings and secrets of their experience, and that of their people. They share glimpses of the Kingdom of God and tell me of lives transformed, dreams fulfilled, pain endured.

Am I rich or poor?

THREE

Generous and Faithful Stewards

JESUS WANTS US to be generous givers. He specifically envisions this in many of his teachings, and it is also the indirect consequence of other teachings. When his economic policies are put into effect, the overall result creates a financial condition and a personal orientation which makes generous giving possible. Those whom he encouraged to "sell all" were also instructed to "give alms" (Lk 12:33) and to "distribute to the poor" (Lk 18:22). He encouraged us to make friends for ourselves by means of unrighteous mammon (Lk 16:9) and to invite the poor and the maimed to our dinner parties (Lk 14:13). He wanted the lives of his followers to manifest amazing generosity.

Sometimes he appealed to our own self-interest. "Give and it will be given you; good measure, pressed down, shaken together, running over, will be put into your lap. For the measure you give will be the measure you get back" (Lk 6:38). Here the call to generosity is based on a fundamental insight regarding the nature of human experience—the measure you give will be the measure you get back. We may not always see this, but in the long run, it is a promise which God himself fulfills. Our certainty of this compels us to keep giving.

Much wisdom is hidden within the simplicity of this word. For one thing, he orients our action towards the future. The expectation of future good is the basis for present giving.

This is significant considering the growing awareness in studies of human behavior which show how much our actions are determined by our past experience. We generally treat others as others have treated us. Experiences in childhood and in our own early history are repeated and passed on in the way we respond to life situations. The determining power of this history is so strong in human experience that it often seems we have little choice in shaping the kind of person we shall become. The die is already cast by our history. The impact of the past is not suspended in the lives of those who believe. All of those past experiences, deeply imprinted in our consciousness, are still shaping our response to every situation. But the future lies before us—open and uncharted. And as we look to this future, it can release within us—with God's help—a power of motivation and of action that can overrule the past.

God wants to free us to give, generously, in good measure, pressed down and running over! As we look to him and are confident in his good purpose for us, knowing that the measure we give will be the measure we get back, we discover the courage to step out and share in ways that are otherwise quite beyond us. Jesus wants to teach us generosity.

At times Jesus prompts us to a motive deeper than self-interest—we are to be like God. "Be merciful, even as your Father is merciful" (Lk 6:36). Here he is addressing the many complex and difficult situations in life in which our generosity—if it exists—is not purely voluntary. These situations require the clarity of a more profound motivation. It is relatively easy to be generous when we are free to decide how much to give, when to give, and to whom. If we have any inclination to be a cheerful giver, we will probably manage it under those circumstances. But what if others take us for granted, require of us what we have not chosen to give? What then of our generosity? Yet even under these more difficult circumstances, Jesus wants us to be cheerful givers.

If someone asks you for something, Jesus said you should give it to him (Mt 5:42). If someone wants to borrow something, loan it to him. Even if someone comes and takes away your property without asking, don't try to get it back (Lk 6:30). And if he sues you for your coat, let him have your overcoat as well. In other words give freely and generously to others.

It is particularly in difficult situations that Jesus invites us to act like sons and daughters of the Father. "He makes his sun rise on the evil and on the good, and sends rain on the just and on the unjust" (Mt 5:45). God gives generously to the unjust and so should we. As we give to those who demand it wrongly we "will be sons of the Most High; for he is kind to the ungrateful and the selfish" (Lk 6:35). We should love others as God has loved us. We not only have a future that impells us toward generosity, but we also have a past, a history with God which speaks the same language. Give as it has been given to you or give and it will be given! Take it either way, take it both ways—in any case, open the doors and let others share what God has given you!

Jesus' teaching about loans is an example of how far he wants us to go with this generosity. It is also significant in showing how he connected with the Old Testament's economic teaching. Jesus did not pick up and repeat the Old Testament prohibition regarding charging interest on loans. Instead, he went beyond the Old Testament and said we should not even insist on getting the principal back! "Even sinners lend to sinners, to receive as much again. But love your enemies, do good, and lend, expecting nothing in return" (Lk 6:34). That is how far he wants us to go in being generous even to those who take advantage of us.

Jesus not only taught about giving to the poor, he demonstrated it in his own life with the disciples. We glimpse this in an incident which took place on his final evening with them. When Judas left the upper room and went out to find his co-conspirators, some of the other disciples "thought that, because Judas had the money box, Jesus was telling him . . . that he should give something to the poor" (Jn 13:29). Giving alms to the poor was such a regular practice for Jesus in his life with the Twelve, that their minds naturally turned to this when Judas made an unexplained departure. So Jesus practiced economic generosity as well as teaching about it.

Jesus makes a final point about giving, without which many

of the other teachings would lose their intended blessing. "When you give alms, sound no trumpet before you, as the hypocrites do in the synagogues and in the streets, that they may be praised by men. Truly, I say to you, they have their reward. But when you give alms, do not let your left hand know what your right hand is doing, so that your alms may be in secret; and your Father who sees in secret will reward you" (Mt 6:2-4). Jesus wants giving that is truly free. Some people are willing to donate money, but only in exchange for a social-emotional reward. We have all seen examples of this kind of conspicuous giving, which leads to paternalism and manipulation—gifts given with strings attached or just for public relations purposes. Givers who want a personal payoff can be as burdensome as those who are stingy with the money itself. Instead, Jesus wants our gifts to be true gifts, with no strings attached. How refreshing it is to be on the receiving end of such gifts! And how blessed it is to be on the giving end!

Not only are we to avoid doing our giving so that others will see, but we are not to keep a close account of it ourselves. "Do not let your left hand know what your right hand is doing" (Mt 6:3). Some have noted that it takes two hands to count your money. If you just grab some with one hand and give it away you will not know how much has gone out. Regardless of whether that was his specific intent, it's clear that Jesus is talking about our own personal awareness. Keeping a careful internal record of all of our good deeds will in itself limit the freedom of giving which Jesus intends.

More With Less

One day when he and his disciples were at the temple in Jerusalem, Jesus noticed people putting their money into the temple offering box. He saw the rich putting in their gifts, some of them no doubt substantial ones, for many of the Jews of that time regularly gave one-tenth of all that they earned (Lk 18:12). And he also saw a poor widow put in two copper coins. Seeing this he turned to his disciples and said, "Truly, I tell you, this poor widow has put in more than all of them; for they all contributed out of their abundance, but she out of her poverty put in all the living that she had" (Lk 21:3-4).

How can it be that a couple of pennies put in by a poor widow actually constitute "more" than all the substantial gifts of the well-to-do? Yet that is how it adds up in the Kingdom of God. Her one gift exceeded in value all that was contributed by the others that day. She certainly did more with less.

Jesus seems to suggest that in the Kingdom perspective, the value of a gift is determined by its value to the giver, which apparently has more to do with how much is leftover than with how much has been given. The gifts of the rich may have been of great value, but the gift of the poor widow exceeded them all, because she put in her whole living.

This incident clarifies several important considerations. First, the potential for giving "much" is open to everyone, even to the very poor. In the world economic system, the poor never have this opportunity. Only the rich can afford to be very generous or to make large investments. But in the Kingdom of God, the poorest widow can become a big giver and therefore a big investor in the Kingdom. This is important because being able to give something of value is one of the greatest things in life. It is, in fact, as Jesus pointed out, "more blessed to give than to receive" (Acts 20:35). People who are always on the receiving end and who feel that they have nothing important to give are among the most impoverished of human beings. So it is good to know that even the very poor can give "much." And the "much" which they can give is precisely in the realm of economics. It is not that wealthy persons can give money, while the poor must think of something else. The poor can also give money. And in the economics of the Kingdom, the poor widows of the earth can invest as much, or more, than the richest philanthropist. What a tremendous opportunity at the disposal of the poor! They can become very rich indeed, in the treasures of the Kingdom.

The Macedonian Christians understood this. "We want you to know, brethren, about the grace of God which has been shown in the churches of Macedonia, for in a severe test of affliction, their abundance of joy and their extreme poverty have overflowed in a wealth of liberality on their part. For they gave according to their means, as I can testify, and beyond their means, of their own free will, begging us earnestly for the favor of taking part in the relief of the saints" (2 Cor 8:1-4).

One of the greatest gifts which we can offer the poor, as well as the rich, is the discovery of the blessing of such generous giving. What the poor can give is of great significance in the Kingdom of God. And the economically poor need to know this. They also need to know that they can "afford" to give. When one is extremely poor it always seems that every penny is necessary for survival. How can we spare anything for others? That is the very reason that the story of the poor widow finds its place in the Gospels! She felt free to put in her pennies—her whole living! And Jesus commended her for doing so.

Many of us would think she went too far. How would her own needs be met? Was it right for her to put in everything that she had? We might be inclined to frown on such reckless giving. But Jesus wasn't worried. In his eyes she had not gone too far or put in too much. He knew that the heavenly Father would care for the needs of a widow like this. He had no reason to be concerned about her welfare. Instead, he was excited about her faith and her valuable contribution to the Kingdom.

What great things can be accomplished with so little in the work of God's Kingdom! How wonderful it is that we are free to invest so fully, even to give all that we have! In a world beset with economic poverty and inadequate resources it is good to know that we can do "more with less."

Our Father in Heaven

Jesus wants to show us the Father. He came to reveal how much God loves us and how intimately he is involved in our personal lives. Jesus also sought to show us how directly we can speak to God and bring our needs before him.

The revelation of God as our loving Father is at the heart of what is new and wonderful in Jesus. Israel had come to know a great deal about God and his ways with men, but until the coming of Jesus no one had been able to grasp or reveal the depth of the Father's love and care. And even to this day, in spite of all that we have seen and heard, it is difficult for us to really comprehend how much the Father loves us and how closely he is involved in everything that happens to us. So Jesus used the analogy of parenthood to help us understand the love of God. "What father among you," he asked, "if his son asks for a fish, will instead of a fish give him a serpent; or if he asks for an egg, will give him a scorpion?" (Lk 11:11). The parent-child relationship often plumbs deeply into the mystery of covenant love and self-giving compassion. We really care about our children. We want the best for them. We are prepared to make great sacrifices so that their needs can be met and their welfare established. Parental love runs deep.

Realizing how much we care about our children, how unthinkable it would be to neglect their basic needs, how ready we are to answer requests—when they are reasonable—Jesus invites us to glimpse the heavenly Father's love. He puts God into this picture of earthly fatherhood, while insisting that God's love is "much more." "If you then, who are evil, know how to give good gifts to your children, how much more will your Father who is in heaven give good things to those who ask him!" (Mt 7:11).

Jesus did not overlook the evil that exists in relationships with earthly fathers. He mentions it explicitly—"If you then, who are evil." Our own generation may be more aware than many previous generations of the limitations and failures of parents. We have evidence on every hand of parents who neglect and abuse their children. Yet even so, the analogy of human parenthood is a good one. There is still enough awareness in us all, whether from our own experience or from our perception of how it should have been, for us to see the point that Jesus makes.

God Almighty, the Creator of heaven and earth, relates to you and me like a loving Father. He maintains a personal interest. He is totally committed to supply what we need and is more aware than we are of all this involves. We can be as secure and carefree in the Father's love as a young child within the warmth of a secure and stable earthly family. We can approach God as directly and confidently as the child who asks his earthly father for bread! And don't forget the addition of "much more"—much, much more! The human experience of parenting, even when it is working well, is but a pale reflection of the Father's love. His commitment to us, his love, his diligence to every detail goes far beyond anything we have ever seen even in the best human family. That's God!

As a father of five children, I can really understand Jesus at this point! The analogy of parenthood has spoken to me at crucial moments in my life experience. I can put myself in the position of one of my own children and see how I would approach the situation as their father. And then I realize that God is approaching me in the same way, only with much more love! This realization has been liberating and enabling for me in difficult situations.

Jesus also communicated in other ways how intimately God is involved in our lives. He said, "Even the hairs of your head are all numbered" (Mt 10:30). That's not an analogy. It's a statement of fact. And I find it a little surprising. Is it really possible—or necessary—for God to keep such close watch over everything in the universe? Does he really know us that well? Most of us would not be in a position to comment. But if that is how things are done in heaven Jesus should know, and he said it was so. I believe him. God knows the intimate details of your life and mine. He watches over us to the extent that even the hairs of our head are numbered.

Again, Jesus said, "Are not two sparrows sold for a penny? And not one of them will fall to the ground without your Father's will" (Mt 10:29). Yes, it's hard to imagine that God is that personally involved in what happens to every sparrow throughout the whole earth. But that is what Jesus said. God, the loving Father, attends to the welfare of all his creatures, far more than we realize.

We are to look at the way human parents care for their

children, and then add "much more." We are to look around and see how God cares for all his creation, and again we are to add "much more." Jesus used the most dramatic illustrations imaginable to articulate for us how intimately God cares for the universe. And it is in the strength of this knowledge that he invites us to trust God for our daily bread. "Are you not of much more value?" (Mt 6:26; Mt 10:31) is the recurring question. If God so cares for the rest of creation, will he not "much more" (Mt 6:30) care for you?

As Jesus spells out how we are to trust God and relate to him for all that we need, he also encourages us to "ask." That is the context in which the analogy of parenthood occurs in the Gospels—"Ask, and it will be given you; seek, and you will find; knock, and it will be opened to you. For every one who asks receives, and he who seeks finds, and to him who knocks it will be opened. Or what man of you, if his son asks for bread . . ." (Mt 7:7-10). Our relationship to God the Father is not a passive one. We don't simply receive his care and blessing. Instead, we are invited to take an active role in asking and seeking for the things we need. God doesn't need to be informed—remember, he already knows even the number of our hairs. "In praying do not heap up empty phrases as the Gentiles do; for they think that they will be heard for their many words. Do not be like them, for your Father knows what you need before you ask him" (Mt 6:7). He knows what we need, but still he wants us to ask. Parents will understand. There are things we want to give to our children or things we would like to do with our children, but it is so much better and richer when the children desire what we want to give. God our Father wants that kind of open, cooperative relationship. He doesn't want to force things on us. He wants us to ask for them, to desire them.

God fulfills many things in our life whether we ask him to or not. As Paul affirmed, he does "far more abundantly than all that we ask or think" (Eph 3:20). On the other hand, there are some things which God does not do unless we ask him to. The Apostle James reminded us of this: "You do not have because you do not ask. You ask and do not receive, because you ask wrongly, to spend it on your passions" (Jas 4:2-3). When we ask rightly God responds, and many things are accomplished which would not otherwise occur. Our prayers are a vital and necessary part of God's outpouring of love. That is why Jesus taught that we should ask. He urged us to do so because it makes a difference.

For this discussion it is significant to notice that he specifically urged us to ask for our "daily bread" (Mt 6:11). Were it not for this teaching, we might presume that our daily bread is such an obvious necessity of life that God, being committed to our welfare, would take care of this without our constantly mentioning it to him. Why does it need further discussion? Let's simply trust in God and pick up our weekly paycheck! Not so. The trust in God is right; the fact that he knows our need and is committed to supply it is right. But for some reason, God wants us to regularly ask and receive. He wants us to keep reaching out and articulating our trust, actively looking to him to supply our needs, even for something as routine as daily bread.

In the world you learn that you must work for a living. In the Kingdom of God it is important to learn that you must ask God for your daily bread. Of course, we should also work in whatever way God directs, either as "fishers of fish" or as "fishers of men." When we pray for our daily bread, we simply recognize and respond to the way that the bread of the world is actually supplied. It is less by human achievement, and more by divine providence than most men understand.

That Jesus should have included a request for daily bread in his model prayer, immediately following the prayer for the coming of God's Kingdom and the fulfillment of his will on earth as it is in heaven, shows a tremendous sense of balance that I find refreshing. I am grateful that God invites us to participate with him in his grand strategy for creating a new heaven and a new earth in which righteousness dwells. He could have done it by himself. But he invited us to be partners in this great venture and has committed himself to include our thoughts and petitions as a meaningful part of the entire proceeding. So we are to pray for the coming of his Kingdom. Let us do so—with zeal! Yet our mundane earthly existence is also an important concern in heaven. Even though we are only one among so many, and our life is often filled with disappointments and failures, still the supply of our daily bread ranks along with the coming of the Kingdom as a matter of concern in the courts of heaven. We are invited to bring to the Father that prayer also. Let us be bold and do it!

Jesus was careful to put our trust in God for our daily bread in the context of seeking first the Kingdom of God and his righteousness. "The Gentiles seek all these things; and your heavenly Father knows that you need them all. But seek first his kingdom and his righteousness, and all these things shall be yours as well" (Mt 6:32-33). Even though we can ask for bread, that is not to become our primary concern. If we are truly seeking his Kingdom and his righteousness, our lives will be in their proper context, which facilitates the answer to our prayer for daily bread. We will be involved with other brothers and sisters who are also seeking his Kingdom. Our values and desires will be transformed. We will handle our money in a new way. Our willingness to share with others will be greatly enhanced. Our zeal will be directed toward the extension of his Kingdom rather than the pursuit of possessions and a comfortable life. It is in this context that God can and will hear our prayers for daily bread, and in this context he can and will supply our daily bread.

It is significant that nowhere in his teaching does Jesus suggest that we trust our Christian brothers and sisters to supply our needs. This may surprise us, but Jesus' entire teaching is that we trust only in God. It is the Father who will supply our needs. It is important for us to keep our confidence located in God the Father. I have observed in our own community how easy it is for all of us—myself included—to put our confidence in the Christian brotherhood instead of in God. This will be especially true if the brotherhood we are a part of is working well, and the economic teachings of Jesus are taken seriously. If we experience a lot of sharing and mutual aid in the brotherhood, we can mistakenly begin to put confidence in one another. We are not worried about the future, because we know we can count on our brothers and sisters. They will help us out!

This shift in trust, wherever it occurs, detracts from our relationship to God. Besides, no Christian group is strong enough or secure enough to really fulfill the role of provider. Once faith gets refocused horizontally, it will begin to falter. Doubts and fears will arise—as well they might! What human group is a match for the power of worldwide economic forces?

But if God is our economic provider and has said, "I will never fail you nor forsake you" (Heb 13:5), we can confidently say, "What can man do to me?" (Heb 13:6). Our trust is in the Lord God Almighty, maker of heaven and earth! All of Jesus' teaching on economics are grounded in the reality of God as our loving Father. Trust in the Father's care is the fundamental principle that underlies everything else. Jesus wants us to be free from anxiety. He wants us to be free from unnecessary preoccupation with meeting our material needs. He wants us to be free to share what we have. He wants us to be free to move out in mission. He wants us to be free to do whatever he says without fearing the economic consequences. All of this he accomplishes by revealing the Father to us, by making us aware of how much God loves us, how intimately he is involved in our daily lives, how approachable he is in prayer, and how eager he is to provide all that we need.

Well Done, Good Servant

Jesus said our situation is like that of a group of servants or stewards who have been entrusted with their master's affairs while he is away on a long journey (Mt 24; Lk 19). Upon his return, our master will summon each one of us and ask for an account of our stewardship.

It was common social practice in biblical times to have servants or stewards who assume the role of business manager on the owner's behalf. Joseph in the house of Potiphar in Egypt illustrates this relationship. Potiphar purchased Joseph as a slave from Ishmaelite traders, but when he saw how gifted

Joseph was, and how God blessed everything he did, Potiphar gave him increasing responsibility. Eventually, he made Joseph his "overseer," and placed him "over all that he had" (Gn 39:5). Even though Potiphar was the owner, and Joseph was accountable to him, in the everyday management of Potiphar's affairs, Joseph his steward took full control. "So he left all that he had in Joseph's charge; and having him he had no concern for anything but the food which he ate" (Gn 39:6). Joseph was an excellent manager, a good steward, and the Lord blessed his endeavors.

In what sense are we in that kind of relationship to God? First, a sense of stewardship helps us remember that we are not owners. God is. We have simply been entrusted with the management and care of his property. A lively sense that the things which we possess do not really belong to us will help us keep a clearer vision of what we are trying to do. But God has entrusted management and control of his affairs into our hands. It does seem like the Master has gone on a long journey. This is a useful way to picture the present situation of the church in the world. To a very large extent, the Master's affairs are in our hands. We are asked to make decisions and to see that all things are properly cared for. We are his stewards. The welfare of his household and property are under our oversight. We represent him and care for his interests.

The parable of the master and his stewards also describes our situation in terms of time. In fact, in Luke's Gospel we are told that Jesus introduced this story because his disciples thought the Kingdom of God was to appear immediately (19:11). Here and elsewhere Jesus addresses the particular temptation of thinking that the master's return has been "delayed" or put off indefinitely. A steward who loses the expectation of his master's return is prone to mistreat his fellow servants and neglect his duties (Mt 24:48-49). So one primary purpose of the stewardship concept is to help us understand that there will be some delay in the fulfillment of all God's purposes and to give us a picture of what our role should be in the intervening time.

For many, however, the problem which Jesus was addressing has reversed itself. The coming of the Kingdom has been so long delayed that few are expecting it immediately. For most Christians, this expectation has faded. Thus, the story may be useful in our time to remind us all that the master did eventually return. Our Master likewise shall return, and we should be looking for his coming. For those who have lost a sense of his return, the concept of stewardship is a good reminder that though delayed his return is certain. Thus the time dimension of our stewardship is important, at both ends of the spectrum of expectation.

Jesus uses this story, with its concept of stewardship and its picture of a master who has gone on a long journey, to teach us several important things about our own stewardship. First, a good steward has learned how to be faithful in small things. Even the apparently minor details receive his careful consideration. This point is repeated with each one of the faithful stewards, as they come before the master to give a report of their stewardship. "Well done, good and faithful servant; you have been faithful *over a very little*, I will set you over much" (Mt 25:21, 23). This is even more dramatic in Luke's version of the parable, where the amount of money given to each servant was amazingly small—each servant receives only about $20 and is told to trade with this until the master returns. In Matthew's version, one servant received about $5,000, another about $2,000, and the third about $1,000. In both situations, the master gave them relatively small amounts to work with.

To further highlight the significance of being faithful in small things, Jesus says the steward who traded with $20 and earned $200 was given authority over ten cities! The man who produced $100 was given authority over five cities. What a dramatic increase!—this is Gospel mathematics. Jesus emphasizes the importance of being faithful in little things. It makes a great difference in the long run.

The point of the parable is etched unmistakably before us in the experience of the unfaithful steward whose report comes at the end of the parable. He did nothing but protect and return the original amount of money. "I will condemn you out of your own mouth," said the master (Lk 29:22). The unfaithful steward knew that this master expected to get back more than he had given (v. 21), but instead of translating this into action, he translated it into fear. And out of fear, he did nothing but bury the money and then return it to the master. The master was furious, "You wicked and slothful servant! . . . Take the talent from him, and give it to him who has the ten talents. For to every one who has will more be given, and he will have abundance; but from him who has not, even what he has will be taken away" (Mt 25:26, 28-29).

If we are stewards of the Kingdom we need to understand the principles by which this stewardship operates. This parable illustrates two which are of great significance: 1) Little things are often much more important than we realize. These small assignments are the proving ground in which we learn and demonstrate our capacity to handle the Master's affairs. He always starts us out on small projects, but he actually has great things in mind for us. And 2) Faithful stewardship in the Kingdom of God brings unexpected increase. To him who has—even if what he has is relatively small but well proven—will more be given and he will have in abundance. The man who earned $100 will be put in authority over five cities! Let us not miss the significance of what God has put in our care during this intervening time, while "the Master is away!" We often underestimate the significance of the opportunities that are set before us.

Keeping these principles in mind, let us now see how the concept of stewardship applies to our financial life. First, there is some danger that our concept of stewardship will become overly financial. Because the stewardship parables describe a money management situation, it is easy to allow what was used as an illustration to become the substance of the message. There is a tendency to think that good stewardship means to manage our money like the successful steward in the parable, to invest it, do well financially, and cause the overall net-worth to increase five or tenfold. Then when we see the Master he will surely say, "Well done, good servant."

But applying the stewardship concept directly to our financial life overlooks an important step in translating the meaning of the parable for our own experience. In fact, this oversimplified approach can actually lead to the wrong conclusions. Jesus was only using business success as an example to teach a broader point. He wasn't necessarily saying that he wanted us to be successful in business. It is important not to focus the content of our stewardship too narrowly. When Jesus ascended into heaven and transferred the conduct of his ministry on earth to his stewards, he didn't have any money or real estate to distribute. That wasn't the "treasure" which he left behind for the disciples to invest and manage. Instead, he left them with a missionary mandate—the Gospel and the instruction that it should be preached in all nations. A knowledge of God and his Kingdom, a message of the forgiveness of sins, the power of the Holy Spirit, and authority to heal and cast out demons—this is what he distributed among his stewards. He invites us to invest the Gospel and do business for the Kingdom of God. The increase of this treasure, which he will require at his coming, is not in terms of dollars but in terms of fruit that will abide through all eternity.

This broader understanding of "stewardship" was certainly the one communicated to the Apostles. Paul wrote, "This is how one should regard us, as servants of Christ and stewards of the *mysteries of God.* Moreover, it is required of stewards that they be found trustworthy" (1 Cor 4:1-2). Peter also encouraged us to be faithful stewards: "As each has received a gift, employ it for one another, as good stewards of *God's varied grace*: whoever speaks as one who utters oracles of God; whoever renders service, as one who renders it by the strength which God supplies" (1 Pt 4:10-11).

So when we come before the Master and review our stewardship, he will hold us accountable not merely for our money management but for what we have done with the "mysteries of God" entrusted to us. Our management of money is part of our total stewardship, but it is only a sub-point and not necessarily the focal one. In fact, as we've already noted in the parable of the dishonest steward, it is more important to put our money into the service of the Gospel and of other people than to follow the normal business practices of good money management. There certainly is an appropriate place for good bookkeeping, sensible money management, and good administration of our physical assets. But if we are faithful stewards of the Gospel, there will be occasions when caring for the needs of others and expressing the surprising generosity of God will overrule the usual dictates of financial prudence. Faithful stewardship will sometimes involve dispersing our economic assets in order to enhance the eternal riches of the Kingdom. When Jesus speaks of the Last Judgment, he seems to suggest that he will be more interested in how much of our money we gave away or used in service of others, than in how much we have multiplied our original assets. We should manage our money well and conduct economic business in a way that enhances our total ministry for the Kingdom of God. But we need to take care that we bring a broader concept of being faithful stewards of the Gospel.

In the parable of the dishonest steward in Luke 16 Jesus says, "He who is faithful in a very little is faithful also in much; and he who is dishonest in a very little is dishonest also in much. If then you have not been faithful in the unrighteous mammon, who will entrust to you the true riches? And if you have not been faithful in that which is another's who will give you that which is your own?" (vv. 10-13). His point is that faithfulness in economic matters is something "very little" in the Kingdom of God. For many people in the world, what they do with their money is one of the most important questions in life. But in the Kingdom it is a very small thing.

I've seen this in the lives of people who come to our Fellowship. Often, the biggest struggle at the beginning is to give up all of their money. And for guests and friends who want to know more about our Fellowship life, the financial aspect of it often looms large and appears to be one of the major features of our life together. But from a Kingdom of God perspective, it is one of the smaller points, and in terms of Fellowship life, it is one of the smaller points. It is something "very little." Yet because Jesus also says that the "very little" points of stewardship are "very important," we cannot go on to receive a larger stewardship of the true riches of the Kingdom until we have proven our faithfulness in the little things of this world.

We need to deal with the question of economic faithfulness early in our Christian experience. The history of the people of God down through the centuries confirms this. The life stories of persons who have had a key role in the history of the church frequently include an experience with God, early in their lives, in which the question of finances was dealt with profoundly. Early in their Christian experience, they heard the call of God to forsake everything—to sell all—and to trust God and rely upon him for their economic needs. The details vary, but experiences which touch on these issues appear with great regularity in the history of God's dealing with his people. This was true, of course, for St. Francis of Assisi, but also for John Wesley, for missionary leaders like Hudson Taylor, C.T. Studd, and George Mueller, and for more recent leaders like Watchman Nee. Jesus said that faithfulness in these little things is the foundational core around which a larger and more significant ministry can be built.

We need to consider one other dimension of Christian stewardship. By virtue of our place in the original creation, we human beings have been given a divine stewardship over the earth and all of its plants and animals. "So God crhis own image, in the image of God he created him; male and female he created them. And God blessed them, and God said to them, 'Be fruitful and multiply, and fill the earth and subdue it; and have dominion over the fish of the sea and over the birds of the air and over every living thing that moves upon the earth.' And God said, 'Behold, I have given you every plant yielding seed which is upon the face of all the earth, and every tree with seed in its fruit; you shall have them for food' " (Gn 1:27-30). The earth is still under our care. This stewardship has not been suspended, although it has been made more difficult by the sins of mankind. It is not as embracing and enduring a task as the stewardship of redemption, which comes to us in Christ, but stewardship of the earth is included in redemption. We as individuals and groups need to learn how to be good caretakers of the fish, the birds, the animals, and the earth itself.

In the Old Testament concept of Sabbath rest, even the beasts were to get a holiday (Ex 20:9). And once every seven years, the farm land was to have a year of "solemn rest" and lie idle (Lv 25:4). The principles of the holy life applied to creatures and soil as to the life of man himself. For New Testament believers, the principles of the Kingdom of God certainly extend to natural resources and should guide us as we exercise our stewardship over the earth. Jesus sets us free from the drive to accumulate more and more for ourselves which is at the root of much of the pollution and destruction of the earth. As we learn to take what we need and to share the rest, we will be better able to develop reasonable utilization of natural resources.

An understanding of God's intimate concern for every sparrow that falls and every stream that is polluted will give us a proper respect for the wonderful creation which God has made for our life and enjoyment. The more we see life as a gift of the Creator, the more reverently and creatively we will receive and share it. The generosity we learn to exercise with other people will extend towards animals, trees, and the earth itself. Seeking first the Kingdom of God will help to balance priorities as we give ourselves to those tasks that belong to the orders of creation and those that grow out of God's unfolding redemption. Paul expressed the strong connection between these two aspects of our stewardship well when he said, "The creation waits with eager longing for the revealing of the sons of God; for the creation was subjected to futility, not of its own will but by the will of him who subjected it in hope; because the creation itself will be set free from its bondage to decay and obtain the glorious liberty of the children of God. We know that the whole creation has been groaning in travail together until now; and not only the creation, but we ourselves, who have the first fruits of the Spirit, grown inwardly as we wait for adoption as sons, the redemption of our bodies" (Rom 8:19-23).

It is clear that as we pray for the coming of God's Kingdom

and experience even now the foretaste of our redemption, we are involved in a task that touches all of creation, and for which all creation waits. The fulfillment of this task is an eschatological one—our bodies will be resurrected and creation will be freed from its bondage to decay. Although our present stewardship is not so lofty, we care for the earth in anticipation. Our physical bodies and the entire created order must be handled with care and respect because of the place which they occupy in the plan of God, and because of our place in God's plan.

We have now reviewed some of the main teachings of Jesus regarding money. The example of his life is an equally powerful statement of the same totally new approach to economic reality. It was no coincidence that he was born in a stable, that he lived as he did, that the clothing he wore was all that remained of his possessions when he died, and that he was buried in a borrowed tomb. This was all intentional—part of God's revelation. "You know the grace of our Lord Jesus Christ, that though he was rich, yet for your sake he become poor, so that by his poverty you might become rich" (2 Cor 8:9). Jesus voluntarily chose the way of poverty because by so doing he could most clearly open up the riches of heaven to men on earth.

Jesus and the Old Testament

A few reflections about how the economic teaching and example of Jesus relate to the Old Testament background would be appropriate at this point. We have already noted a number of these connections in the course of our survey, but it should be noted at this point that Jesus chose to connect much more strongly with the justice tradition of the Old Testament than with the tithing tradition. His only references to tithing appear in his criticism of faithful tithers who missed the heart of God's message, like the self-righteous Pharisee of Luke 18. He also said, "Woe to you, scribes and Pharisees, hypocrites! for you tithe mint and dill and cummin, and have neglected the weightier matters of the law, justice and mercy and faith; these you ought to have done, without neglecting the others. You blind guides, straining out a gnat and swallowing a camel! (Mt 23:23).

The Pharisees were very zealous tithers—they even gave a tenth of the mint, dill, and cummin which was raised in the garden! But tithing, even to this extent, without an equal zeal for justice is, in the evaluation of Jesus, like straining out gnats and swallowing camels! He does not deny the validity of straining out gnats. This, he said, should not be neglected. But justice comes first. Many Christians today are in danger of making the same mistake. They tithe faithfully but give no attention to questions of economic justice. The relative importance which Jesus attaches to these two dimensions of economic faithfulness deserves our attention.

The famous announcement Jesus made in the synagogue in Nazareth also reveals his connection with the justice tradition of the Old Testament: "The Spirit of the Lord is upon me, because he has anointed me to preach good news to the poor. He has sent me to proclaim release to the captives and recovering of sight to the blind, to set at liberty those who are oppressed, to proclaim the acceptable year of the Lord" (Lk 4:18-19). This quote from Isaiah 61 specifically mentions the features of the Year of Jubilee—good news to the poor, release to the captives, liberty for those who are oppressed—it was a kind of Jubilee proclamation. But the "acceptable year of the Lord" envisioned by the prophet and announced by Jesus goes far beyond the traditional Year of Jubilee and even includes recovering of sight to the blind, which certainly no Old Testament Jubilee ever included. The prophet foretells a Messianic Jubilee which embraces far more than what the people of God had known in earlier centuries. And this is exactly what came to pass in Jesus.

All of the phrases in this Messianic proclamation—good news to the poor, release to the captives—have meanings that go beyond economics. Jesus proclaimed a more profound and comprehensive Jubilee, one in which all sins (i.e., all debts) could be cancelled, all bondages—psychological and spiritual, as well as economic—could be broken and all captives could go free. Yet there is no indication that he meant to leave the economic meaning behind. Indeed, Jesus initiated a kind of open-ended era of economic Jubilee, one facet of the larger Messianic announcement of the "acceptable year of the Lord."

The prophet envisioned an eschatological Year of Jubilee when God's good news would be proclaimed as never before, and this was fulfilled in the coming of Jesus, who rightly claimed, "Today, this scripture has been fulfilled in your hearing" (Lk 4:21). His ministry, by his own choice and declaration, was envisioned in the context of the Old Testament Jubilee. The Old Testament Jubilee was a prototype of the grace-filled generosity which God sets forth in Christ. The economic dimensions of Jubilee are not lost in Christ. He taught, announced, and advocated a Jubilee approach to economics—not just for a year, but for this whole era in which we live. In the Old Testament Year of Jubilee, capital wealth was redistributed by the restoring of families to their original inheritance. In Jesus' proclamation, capital wealth is redistributed because God has chosen to "give us the Kingdom" (Lk 12:32), and we are all going on to our new inheritance.

The continuity between the justice tradition of the Old Testament and the economic vision presented by Jesus is further exemplified by his teaching on loans. The canceling of loans was one of the primary features of the Year of Release as well as the Year of Jubilee.

We have already noted the strong parallel between the Old Testament experience of exodus, wilderness, and promised land,and the New Testament experience of being saved out of the world and invited into the Kingdom of God. Jesus obviously built on the earlier experience of God's people. But while it is important to build on this continuity, we must make Jesus our primary authority in our teaching and understanding of financial matters. This is not true of some contemporary teaching about God's promises of abundance and prosperity. Built almost entirely on Old Testament texts, this teaching omits or neglects many of the most important things which Jesus had to say on the subject. Of course, all of the Old Testament promises are still true, and they are supplemented by Jesus' own strong assurances of God's care and provision. But when Jesus taught about the certainty of God's provision for us, he nearly always linked it with a call to unusual generosity or to the value of traveling light. Apart from Jesus' teaching these Old Testament promises of abundance can create a wrong impression about the total thrust of what God desires for us. The balance in our teaching on economics should reflect the balance that we see in Jesus.

FOUR

The New Testament Church and Finances

WE WILL NOT be surprised by what happened in Jerusalem following Pentecost if we have grasped the strong economic component in the message of Jesus. Jerusalem Christians were simply doing what they had been taught. Since there was such a clear and strong economic side to the teaching of Jesus, it follows that when the church got underway in power, there would be a definite economic aspect to its new life. The economic life of the Jerusalem church strongly confirms the economic teaching of Jesus.

Many persons try to diminish the significance of what happened in Jerusalem by quickly observing that "it didn't last," which reassures them that Jesus' radical approach to economics as demonstrated in Jerusalem is not expected of the rest of us.

This easy dismissal is based, however, on an erroneous reading of what did happen in Jerusalem. I believe that a more careful assessment of what went on there reveals Christian economics of a sort that does continue through the subsequent years of New Testament Christianity and beyond into the later history of the church. It is certainly clear that the other churches did not adopt a common treasury, in which individual finances were completely centralized and communalized. But that is not what happened even in Jerusalem. The assumption that it did over-interprets what is meant by "holding all things in common." Nothing indicates that all 3,000 persons who accepted Christ the first day reorganized their whole economic life into one common, communal system.

We are told that "all who believed were together and had all things in common" (Acts 2:44). But the way this functioned is that "no one said that any of the things which he possessed was his own" (Acts 4:32). Individuals still possessed things, yet they had all things in common. Their attitudes toward economic things were so changed that individual ownership did not define individual use. Everything that everyone owned was available for common use. It didn't matter who possessed it.

Within this context, we are also told that "as many as were possessors of lands or houses sold them, and brought the proceeds of what was sold and laid it at the apostles' feet" (Acts 4:34). It is clear in the Greek text that this describes an ongoing process. Those who had the most were selling it, and those who were in need were receiving assistance. It is likely that the large majority went on with their own resources in the usual way, but with many smaller acts of kindness and sharing. Individual stewardship and control were still operative even though they produced an "in-common" effect. Peter's response to Ananias confirms this. "While it remained unsold, did it not remain your own? And after it was sold, was it not at your disposal?" (Acts 5:4). This was the manner in which the early church held all things in common. It was a loosely organized redistribution, not a total communalization of financial management. Furthermore, attention to the numbers of people supports this conclusion. Within a very short period of time the number of believers had grown to 5,000 men (Acts 4:4). If you add women and children, you would need to project a total community of at least 20,000 or 30,000 persons. Yet when the apostles wanted to delegate the "daily distribution" to other men, they only chose seven persons. Seven men could not handle corporate finances and daily food distribution for 20,000 people. But they could handle the more limited redistribution from rich to poor which was taking place on a daily basis.

What they had, then, in Jerusalem was a very generous

sharing of resources with so strong an impact that they could say there wasn't a needy person among them (Acts 4:34). Their attitudes had so changed that no one said the things he possessed were his own. In this way they held all things in common. There were many poor in Jerusalem among the believers, but as the Messianic Jubilee got underway, not a needy one was overlooked. This truly was good news for the poor!

Another aspect of the Jerusalem experience reflects the radical message of Jesus. They were selling houses and lands and using this money to buy food and clothing. They were using capital wealth to pay current running expenses. Now, that is radical! It goes against good business management principles. But like the dishonest steward of Luke 16, these Jerusalem believers had devised a short-term economic heresy which had a tremendous long-term Kingdom of God result! It takes a strong sense of eschatology—not necessarily its imminence but the *importance* of the age to come—to sell houses and lands to buy groceries. But that is what they were doing. And they were freely distributing these funds to any one who had need.

There is ample evidence to suggest that a similar kind of generous sharing took place in other parts of the early church as well. In Thessalonica there were people who wanted to live off the church without working. "We hear that some of you are living in idleness, mere busybodies, not doing any work" (2 Thes 3:11). Paul reminds them of the principle he laid out at the beginning of his ministry there, "If any one will not work, let him not eat" (2 Thes 3:10). Both the original teaching and the subsequent problem indicate that a high level of economic sharing was anticipated and realized. You cannot have a problem of this sort unless there is a lot of financial sharing. In fact, many churches today could not have this problem of members wanting to live off the church without working. It doesn't even come up. The government has this problem now, because the state is doing more than the church in meeting the needs of the poor.

Another small but significant reflection in Romans 12:13

shows how much such generous sharing was to be expected among the early Christians: "Contribute to the needs of the saints, practice hospitality." The Greek verb translated in the Revised Standard Version as "contribute" is a form of the word "koine," which means to make things common. This is exactly the same term which is used in Acts to describe the generous sharing in Jerusalem. A more exact translation for Romans 12:13 could read, "With regard to the needs of the saints, practice making all things common!" Paul recommends that believers in Rome, as in Jerusalem, should practice making things common. Ownership is not the controlling factor in the use of a possession. The needs of a brother take priority over the fact of ownership. The fact that Paul advocates the same concept as was used in Jerusalem, writing so many years later to a church in another part of the Empire, suggests that generous sharing of possessions was a continuing feature of the life-style of the early church.

The Apostle John did not forget this principle either, as years went by and the church expanded. He could still write, many decades after the Jerusalem church began, "If any one has the world's goods and sees his brother in need, and yet closes his heart against him, how does God's love dwell in him? Little children, let us not love in word or speech but in deed and in truth" (1 Jn 3:17-18). John does not hesitate to attach the strongest possible theological significance to the practice of sharing your goods with a brother. Refusing to share, in John's mind, repudiates the reality of God's love dwelling in you. Such strong advocacy of economic sharing would make no sense unless this was an accepted part of the teaching and practice of the church.

When Paul addressed the Corinthians concerning the collection being gathered for the Jerusalem church, he holds up the voluntary poverty of Jesus as an example. "He was rich, yet for your sake he became poor" (2 Cor 8:9). Paul has already noted the "overflowing wealth of liberality" of the Macedonians in spite of their "extreme poverty" (8:1-4). The Macedonians had certainly caught the Kingdom vision of generous sharing, and Paul urges the Corinthian believers to do the same.

Paul also says, "I do not mean that others should be eased and you burdened, but that as a matter of equality your abundance at the present time should supply their want, so that their abundance may supply your want, that there may be equality. As it is written, 'He who gathered much had nothing over, and he who gathered little had no lack' " (2 Cor 8:13-15). These are strong words; here Paul advocates equality as the goal for economic life in the church. There will be times when each of us will be in a position to give, and other times when we will need to receive. Paul advocates a free flow of available resources so that in both of these situations an overall equality may be attained. The abundance of certain persons or churches should be channeled to others who are in need to achieve equality.

Paul then refers to the experience of Israel in the wilderness. Even at that early date, God was trying to teach his people equality. We have already noted that he was trying to teach his people to trust him to supply their needs. But he also wanted Israel to know that the things which he supplied were to be distributed equally among the people. This is very clear in God's plan—an ingenious one, when you think about it. God instructed the people to gather only as much as they could eat: " 'Gather of it, every man of you, as much as he can eat; you shall take an omer apiece, according to the number of persons whom each of you has in his tent.' And the people of Israel did so, they gathered, some more, some less. But when they measured it with an omer, he that gathered much had nothing over, and he that gathered little had no lack" (Ex 16:16-18).

Whether this equalization was achieved miraculously or through a process of redistribution is not clear, but the essential point is the same. God designed a system of equality. He who gathered much had nothing left over, he who gathered little had no lack. And to further reinforce this principle, as well as the principle of faith, God designed it so that nothing could be saved from day to day. But even though the people were told not to leave anything until the next day, "they did not listen to Moses; some left part of it till the morning, and it bred worms and became foul" (v. 20). Thus inequality through accumulation, as well as inequality because of work, skill, or good fortune, was ruled out in God's plan. God's system guaranteed equality. This was part of the teaching experience in the wilderness.

God set up a practical demonstration of how economics should function within the community of faith. Many years later, Paul affirms that this concept is still valid within the New Covenant people of God. But this vigorous equality is no longer forced on us—God now wants us to achieve it voluntarily. But the overall goal is still the same: those who gather much should have nothing left over and those who gather little should have no lack. Generous sharing certainly did not—and should not—end in Jerusalem. For New Testament Christians this generous sharing of goods constituted an important aspect of their relationship to God. It was worship, sacrifice. It was the New Testament fulfillment of what used to take place in the temple as priests offered up sacrifices to God. Paul wrote, "I am filled, having received from Epaphroditus the gifts you sent, a fragrant offering, a sacrifice acceptable and pleasing to God" (Phil 4:18). Similarly, in Hebrews we read, "Do not neglect to do good and to share what you have, for such sacrifices are pleasing to God" (Heb 13:16). The sharing of goods among brothers and sisters in the Christian movement is an exercise of faith, a testimony to God, a religious action of the highest order. Such sharing is in fact a "sacrament" to God, a fragrant offering, acceptable, and pleasing in the Father's presence.

In summary, the New Testament churches did not have a communal treasury with centralized decisions and control of finances—various texts reflect individual control and individual decisions. But they did have a spirit of love and brotherhood which resulted in a pattern of redistribution that had the practical effect of making things common. Jesus and the Twelve apparently functioned with a common purse. The kind of communal treasury that has been characteristic of religious communities down through the centuries resembles this in some respects. But the churches typically utilized a loosely structured sharing of extensive proportions.

The Church in Early Centuries

This strong thrust towards sharing of goods continues in the church even beyond the close of the New Testament era. Let me share a few examples. The Didache, a widely recognized document written towards the end of the first century and entitled "The Teaching of the Twelve Apostles," states: "Do not be one who stretches out his hands to receive but closes them when it comes to giving. If you have earned something by the work of your hands, pass it on as a ransom for your sins. Do not hesitate to give, and do not grumble when giving, for you will know who is the glorious giver of your reward. Do not turn away from those who are in need but share all things in common. Share all things in common with your brother. Do not claim anything as your own for if we have fellowship in the immortal, how much more in perishable things"[1] [*The Early Christians,* Eberhard Arnold, (Rifton, New York: Plough Publishing House), p. 183].

Justin Martyr, writing around 140 A.D., explained in his First Apology, "We ourselves who used to have pleasure in impure things, now cling to chastity alone. We who dabbled in the arts of magic, now consecrate ourselves to the good and unbegotten God. We who formerly treasured money and possessions more than anything else now hand over everything we have to a treasury for all and share it with everyone who needs it"[2] [*The Early Christians,* Arnold, p. 100].

Tertullian, writing at the end of the second century, described the church of his time as follows: "The most proved men preside, the elders, we call them. They have attained this honor only through their good name, never through the use of money. For nothing that is of God can be bought for money.

Even though we have a kind of cash box, the money does not come from admission fees, as when one buys membership or position in a society; that would be like buying religion. Rather every man contributes something once a month, or whenever he wishes to, and only if he wishes to, and if he can, for no one is forced. But everyone gives his share willingly. These contributions might be called the deposit funds of fellowship with God, as they are not spent on banquets or drinking parties or gluttony, rather they are used to feed and bury the poor, for boys and girls without means and without parents, to help them . . . for shipwrecked sailors, for those doing forced labor in the mines, or banished on islands or imprisoned, provided they suffer for the sake of God's fellowship. . . . But even such acts of great love set a stain on us in the eyes of some people. . . . They get excited because we are called by the name of "brother." . . . Maybe we are not considered quite legitimate because our brotherliness is not loudly declaimed in a tragedy or because we are brothers with regard to our family possessions too, at which point your brotherliness ceases to exist, as a rule. We who are inwardly bound together in spirit and soul have no hesitation in surrendering our property. We hold everything in common except our wives. At this point we dissolve our community. And this is precisely the one point in which the rest of men practice community"[3] [*The Early Christians,* Arnold, pp. 111-12].

Did it end in Jerusalem? Obviously not. Extensive sharing of goods, even to the point of holding all things in common, pervaded the experience of the New Testament and post-New Testament churches. This practice has found strong expression in various parts of the church down through the years. The monastic and religious orders are one of the most notable example. The Radical Reformation of the 16th century is another. Within the Anabaptist movement of that time, one large section of the renewal set up common bruderhofs where all lived together in common, and in other parts of the Anabaptist movement—as with the early church—their sharing of possessions was so real that others described it as holding all things in common. Some of the Moravian communities also manifested much sharing of goods. And during the 19th and 20th centuries there have been many communal Christian groups in the United States and in other parts of the world.

FIVE

Some Current Questions

I WOULD NOW like to discuss several areas of contemporary economic practice in which I believe the biblical witness needs a fresh hearing. These are indebtedness, insurance, missionary strategy, and covenant economics. There are biblical teachings that touch directly on some of these subjects, although the matter of insurance is not mentioned at all since it is a recent invention, and what follows is my interpretation and application of them. I am drawing conclusions which are not clearly spelled out in scripture. These may not be the right conclusions, or the only ones, but I offer them for your prayerful consideration. If what I suggest can commend itself as at least one legitimate and worthy application of the biblical teaching, it may open some new options for some of God's people.

Owe No One Anything

Tucked away in Paul's letter to the Romans we find this intriguing statement: "Owe no one anything, except to love one another; for he who loves his neighbor has fulfilled the law" (Rom 13:8).

Throughout the history of the church there have been a number of serious Christians who have noticed this word and concluded that they should avoid all forms of indebtedness. Others have hesitated to draw such sweeping conclusions from such a brief and isolated reference, and in most parts of the church there has been no particular teaching against indebtedness. There are therefore large numbers of Christians who borrow and lend in exactly the same manner as their unbelieving contemporaries. I believe that Christians should be warned against debts and that Paul's admonition should be taken more seriously. What is the biblical evidence?

The association between debts and slavery in the instructions regarding a Year of Release (Dt 15) is more than coincidental. Neither a debtor nor a slave is free to reap the full return of his own labor or to utilize it however he chooses. Part or all of what they produce is owed to another. And in both cases, someone (in the case of a slave, his owner) has paid money at the beginning of the relationship in exchange for the pledge of service or cash. Slavery and indebtedness differ greatly in the *portion* which is owed to another person, but the fundamental structure of both relationships has striking similarities. And in the biblical Year of Release, both conditions are given the same resolution: cancel the debts, let the salves go free (Dt 15:2, 12).

This same section of scripture contains a perspective on indebtedness which is worth considering: "The Lord your God will bless you, as he promised you, and you shall lend to many nations, but you shall not borrow; and you shall rule over many nations, but they shall not rule over you" (Dt 15:6).

Two important points are made here. First, when the Lord is blessing us we will lend to others, but we will not borrow from others. This could be understood simply to mean that when God is blessing us we will become so prosperous that we will never need to borrow. While this is part of the intended meaning, the parallelism concerning rule shows that the writer thought there was much more at stake. Second, this scripture says that when we borrow from others, we give them "rule" over us. In other words, when we owe money to others, they have a certain control over us. We are not completely our own person, able to move and decide as we wish. The one to whom we owe money has a certain claim upon us. This is the most obvious similarity between slavery and indebtedness. If we have debts, we are not completely free. Proverbs makes this point even more clearly: "The rich rules over the poor, and the borrower is the slave of the lender" (Prv 22:7). Several Old Testament passages reflect the idea that God's people will lend but not borrow. Deuteronomy 28, which lists the blessings and curses following obedience or disobedience to God's commands, states that when God's people are obedient they will be lenders (v. 12), and when they are disobedient they will become borrowers (v. 44). Psalm 37 describes "the righteous" as one who is "ever giving liberally and lending" (v. 26), and the "wicked" as one who "borrows" and "cannot pay back" (v. 21). Again, in Psalm 112, "It is well with a man who deals generously and lends, who conducts his affairs with justice" (v. 5). We shouldn't make too much of these scattered references, but they are worth considering.

In the New Testament, it is significant to see where borrowers appear in the teaching of Jesus. Whenever the subject comes up, disciples are pictured in the role of lenders, while borrowers appear along with enemies in the list of those who take advantage of you, those who sue you and otherwise oppress you (Mt 5; Lk 6). Jesus doesn't say that his disciples should not be borrowers; neither does he say that we should not be thieves or Roman imperialists. The association should be considered.

What do enemies, thieves, imperialists, the ungrateful, and the selfish all have in common with those who borrow? The former all impinge upon your freedom, well-being, time, property, or safety because of their own self-interest and at your expense. Likewise, the man who comes to borrow your money wants to use your resources to further his own project; his self-interest is impinging upon yours. He is asking you to make a sacrifice to serve his own well-being. He wants to get ahead at your expense. In the modern world, we balance this by charging interest, which makes it more acceptable and in fact often turns the loan to the lender's advantage. But this creates other problems, which I will discuss later.

This raises another question: Why isn't the man who is borrowing money willing to operate with what he has? Why does he find it necessary to reach out for more resources than are already at his disposal? Throughout scripture contentment with what you have and operating within the limits of your own resources is an important spiritual issue. It is addressed in the commandment against covetousness (Ex 20:17). In the New Testament we are repeatedly encouraged to be content with what we have: "Keep your life free from love of money, and be content with what you have" (Heb 13:5); "There is great gain in godliness with contentment; for we brought nothing into the world, and we cannot take anything out of the world; but if we have food and clothing, with these we shall be content" (1 Tm 6:6-8). (Usually the person borrowing money isn't content with food and clothing.) And of himself Paul testified, "I have learned, in whatever state I am, to be content. I know how to be abased, and I know how to abound; in any and all circumstances I have learned the secret of facing plenty and hunger, abundance and want" (Phil 4:11-12). If Christians today were content with whatever circumstances God allowed to come into their lives, what would be the reason for borrowing?

When we borrow, we are reaching out for more. We want to move faster, do better, accomplish more than we could without borrowing. But if we were content to operate at whatever level our circumstances afforded, the need for borrowing would be eliminated.

Let's look at the same question from a positive viewpoint. We've been told, in a dozen different ways, "Whatever you ask in my name, I will do it, that the Father may be glorified in the Son. If you ask anything in my name, I will do it" (Jn 14:13-14). If our need or project is legitimate, why can't we simply ask God for the necessary resources and expect to receive them? If we want to move faster, accomplish more, do better, why not ask God for the resources to do so? He is eager and ready to respond. We have much to learn about asking in faith and receiving his blessing. And if we ask, but do not receive, perhaps the project is ill-conceived. Can we take no for an answer and still be content? If we borrow, we withhold from God opportunities to bless us and supply our needs. And sometimes we may deny him the opportunity to say no to a project.

James adds this: "Come now, you who say, 'Today or tomorrow we will go into such and such a town and spend a year there and trade and get gain'; whereas you do not know about tomorrow. What is your life? For you are a mist that appears for a little time and then vanishes. Instead you ought to say, 'If the Lord wills, we shall live and we shall do this or that.' As it is, you boast in your arrogance. All such boasting is evil. Whoever knows what is right to do and fails to do it, for him it is sin" (Jas 4:13-17).

Often when we borrow money we enter into a process which is almost exactly that which James condemns. We project our activities for the coming year. We predict that they will be profitable. We estimate how much profit we will generate. And we pledge ourselves to actually achieve the projected profit and to pay our creditor the agreed upon amount.

What's wrong with this? It doesn't sufficiently account for the uncertainties of life. We as Christians need to remain flexible, aware of how tenuous and uncertain our life is and how much it depends upon God's grace and God's direction. One of the biggest problems with borrowing money is that we make predictions about our future and give these predictions a degree of certainty which is beyond our knowledge.

Many Christians have put themselves under a great deal of pressure through debt. If things do not go as planned, we must rush about to try to cover the bases. Often we find ourselves unable to flow with events—with reality—as they are actually occurring, because we have pledged ourselves to a reality that does not exist. By sheer willpower and hard work, we attempt to make reality conform to our plan. Alas, this can have detrimental effects upon our spiritual life. As Paul warned, "Those who desire to be rich . . . fall into many senseless and hurtful desires that plunge men into ruin and destruction" (1 Tm 6:9).

Other times, Christians find themselves unable to move out

in mission, to accept some new assignment or challenge from the Lord—even though their heart desires it—because of debts that must be paid. When we promise to repay, we often do not anticipate the implications the commitment to repay someone will have on our future life and experience. We surrender some control, we pledge some portion of our future life and resources, to someone other than the Lord.

One further point. If we have legitimate needs or good Kingdom of God ideas which require additional funds, in addition to taking this to the Lord in prayer, we should share it with other Christian brothers and sisters. If they have caught the message of Jesus regarding economic generosity, there is a good chance that they will simply give us what we need. Or, if it seems wiser, these fellow Christians may put their gift in the form of a loan. If they follow biblical teaching, they would not charge interest, and the return of the principal would be somewhat optional. Thus repayment of the loan would certainly fall within the framework set by James—"if the Lord wills." If some unexpected circumstances or unforeseen calling of the Lord deferred or cancelled repayment of the loan, those Christian brothers and sisters should have a way of accepting this without difficulty. So if we go to our Christian brothers and sisters and use biblical principles, we can maintain the necessary flexibility and humility before God.

Unfortunately, many Christian individuals and organizations do not operate on these terms. And when we go to secular lending institutions this much "grace" is unthinkable. But still, when we have legitimate needs, taking them to God and to our Christian brothers and sisters should be our preference. Many Christians seem to find it easier to present their needs to a secular banker, and they often seem to get better results! All of that could change if we had a vision for it.

In addition to scripture's general caution against borrowing money, there are serious biblical questions about charging interest on loans. I believe a teaching against interest should be recovered by the church in our time. Significantly, throughout the first ten centuries of the Christian era, it was generally accepted by most, if not all, Christians, that charging interest on loans was contrary to the Christian way of life.

But what about business? So much of our modern world of commerce and industry is built upon the foundation of borrowed capital. Should Christians let others use their money without interest if it is being used to generate income? If a Christian puts up some of the money to finance a business, shouldn't he share in the returns of the business? Or must a faithful Christian avoid involvement in all such capitalistic schemes?

There certainly are ways for Christians to be involved in the commerce and industry of our time. There is nothing wrong with pooling capital from various sources in order to operate a business. Christians should be able to participate in this process without problems of conscience, and it is obviously appropriate for those who contribute capital to have some share in the profits. However, I believe that Christians could develop alternative ways of structuring and administering this process if we had a greater sensitivity to some of the biblical concerns about interest and loans. For instance, various forms of joint ownership through purchase of stock avoid some of the problems inherent in a loan with fixed interest and promise to repay.

In the experience of our Fellowship over the past twenty-five years, we have sought to follow a policy of avoiding debt, and this has worked out amazingly well. One major exception to this policy has been our purchasing of houses and apartment buildings with mortgage loans. At several points, we prayerfully evaluated our policy regarding these mortgages, and each time we did, it seemed the Lord said that we should continue in this way. So even though we see it as a variation from our general approach, we have continued to operate in this manner.

In trying to understand the meaning of this experience we have noted several ways in which a mortgage loan is somewhat unique in comparison to other loans. In particular, it has a carefully worked out "escape" clause in the form of real estate equity. The lender carefully evaluates the property and loans only as much as he would be willing to lose in exchange for taking over control of the property. This speaks somewhat to the issue of the uncertain future and the nature of our promise to repay—if the borrower cannot fulfill his part of the agreement, there is an agreed upon way to resolve the problem. Even this, however, does not answer all of the questions, since these arrangements would not satisfy the lender if property values plunged drastically, as in a severe depression.

Even though the mortgage loan retains some of the problematic features of indebtedness, we perceive the mortgage purchase of housing as a particular form of property ownership which is mid-way between renting and owning a house. In the mortgage situation, we make monthly payments to the bank—similar to any other rental situation—since they own a goodly portion of the property, but we achieve a greater measure of flexibility in how the property is maintained and utilized. For people who are trying to maintain a moderate standard of living, this has seemed like a good mid-term solution, providing some of the flexibility of ownership without all of the accumulated wealth necessary for complete ownership.

Of course, in the case of a severe economic collapse we might find ourselves in a position where we could not make the payments and would eventually lose our properties. But should something like this ever take place, we believe that God will help us to be resourceful and will meet our needs. There is a good possibility that we could make payments, even in difficult times, with God's help. On the other hand, since we have already renounced all that we have and are not trying to lay up for ourselves treasures on earth, we remain ready to lose everything. Even that would be acceptable. In such a situation, we would expect God to meet our needs and would find other places to live. The main problem then would be the disappointment of our lenders, to whom we have both an economic and a moral obligation, and we may have no way of adequately compensating them for their loss. That's one problem for which we have no solution, except as God would reveal it.

Owe no one anything, except to love one another. Perhaps there is more of a biblical rationale for refusing indebtedness than many Christians realize. Paul's word in Romans actually sums it up amazingly well. If we take seriously the claims of love that are already upon us, what is left over to pledge to anyone else? We are already committed to the hilt. If we can earn more than we need, our love for others has already placed claims upon that surplus. The debt of love—which we already owe—is enough. Let us not promise more.

Insurance

The place that insurance occupies in our lives—how and why we participate in it—deserves careful evaluation in any Christian approach to contemporary economics. I want to question some of the standard assumptions. In doing so, I want to clearly recognize that this is a difficult and complex area. It is not addressed specifically in any biblical teaching, since insurance companies didn't exist in ancient times. Thus, any application of biblical teaching in the matter of insurance is a matter of interpretation and judgment. Our own limitations and perspectives enter this picture. And in matters of this kind, it is particularly obvious that we need the testing and insight of other Christians.

Explicitly recognizing these limitations, I want to offer my own understanding of insurance as a contribution to Christian dialogue on the subject. It seems to me that insurance may be one of the most blatant forms of mammonism in contemporary society.

The power of an insurance company resides primarily in large accumulated financial reserves. The insurance company represents money—lots of money. It offers the security that comes through having lots of money. By having a contract with the insurance company, individuals who do not have big financial reserves themselves are able to enjoy the security and protection of financial reserves that belong to someone else. In return for this protection, they agree to "serve" the company by means of regular payments.

Isn't this just the very thing Jesus spoke against—looking for security in lots of money and confidence for the future in strong financial resources? Didn't he say that this was both unwise and unnecessary? And what would it mean to "serve mammon" if it is not to place so much of our sense of confidence and security in a set of relationships that derive their strength from great amounts of accumulated wealth?

A Christian alternative to insurance would involve trusting in God for our protection and for the supply of our future needs, and working out relationships of sharing and mutual aid among Christian individuals and groups so that emergencies of various sorts could be handled gracefully. A contract with the insurance company to cover these situations resembles, in a theological sense, the alliances Israel made with Egypt and Assyria to assure her national survival. Given the extent of the military dangers, it seemed no longer possible to simply rely upon God and the resources of his people. Safety, survival, and confidence for the future seemed to require an alliance with a worldly power which had the visible capability of warding off potential dangers. So Israel made alliances with worldly powers to secure her safety.

The insurance companies are also worldly powers. They have great resources of the kind that are effective in the world. If one of those big companies has promsied to "deliver" you in case of difficulties, you can feel secure, since any conceivable crisis covered by your contract will not be too big for them to handle. So if you are covered, you are safe. A contract with one of the big worldly powers thus becomes a definite need.

The kings of Israel paid yearly tribute to the kings of Assyria and Egypt in exchange for this "protection." And the big "powers" today expect the same thing. But the prophets pronounced "woe" upon those who "take refuge in the protection of Pharoah, and . . . seek shelter in the shadow of Egypt!" (Is 30:1-2).

Like most things in the world, the insurance companies represent a mixture of good elements and bad. On the one hand, they are performing some very necessary, helpful, and beneficial services. You could even say they represent a secular form of brotherhood and mutual aid. They bring help to persons in distress. They meet large and unexpected needs and keep individuals from being overwhelmed by the requirements of these special circumstances. They provide family support in old age or when the wage earner dies. They gather support from a wide circle and distribute it to those who have the greatest need, and so achieve a measure of sharing and equalization. The impact of large scale losses is shared so that all can help to bear the load. These functions are necessary and good. And in addition to these primary functions, the insurance companies also perform a variety of secondary services, such as encouraging saving and giving good advice.

Many of these positive functions which insurance companies fulfill reflect the origins of the whole concept within the context of Christian faith. The earliest insurance companies were Christian mutual aid organizations. They were set up to facilitate these brotherhood functions within the Christian movement. Once the concept for such mutual aid was demonstrated, its value extended far beyond the Christian church, and insurance became a basic feature in modern industrial society.

In retrospect it seems that the design of the original concept, while doing a good job of lifting up the mutual aid functions, did so without sufficient sensitivity to some of the other economic principles of the Kingdom of God. This produced an undue reliance upon accumulated wealth as the basic principle of operation. Proof that this insurance company model is deficient, from a Kingdom of God point of view, is evident in the history of its development. The concept of insurance quickly became one of the most useful and profitable ideas in the world of mammon. A more thoroughgoing godly approach to mutual aid would not lend itself so readily, and with so little alteration, to becoming a primary instrument in the secular world of business.

The assistance which insurance provides is particularly necessary in the modern world. Two factors, especially, create the need for the services which insurance companies offer. One is the high cost of living and dying in a technological society. Death, retirement, illness, accidents, unemployment, and other possible events have all increased greatly in cost to the point where few individuals and organizations can face the unknown future without the need for assistance. Accidents and potential liabilities have especially increased as the power of our machines and the scope of our relationships have multiplied through technology and organization.

Second, while our needs and costs have multiplied, our social network has diminished. In earlier times, family, clan, and neighborhood resources were brought to bear in assisting individuals in times of crisis. But many individuals and organizations today find themselves with few, if any, committed relationships of the sort that would provide substantial help should they find themselves in crisis or unusual need. So our society "needs the services that insurance companies provide. I do not mean to suggest that the society as a whole could function at this time without the insurance companies. The services which they offer must be supplied in some manner.

However, even though some of these services are needed and helpful, the way in which insurance provides them is problematic from a Christian point of view. The extent to which the whole structure is built upon a confidence in the power of money has already been identified. This unwarranted commercialism can also be seen from another perspective. The kind of caring and sharing that insurance companies approximate is something which we all need, and in God's plan it should arise out of strong personal, family, and community relationships. Yet in our modern world, this kind of care is being bought and sold for a price, and often for a profit.

It is also true that a great deal of the rationale and motivation for insurance revolves around anxiety, a fear of what might happen to us, as we project likely probabilities upon the unrevealed script of future events. Jesus spoke strongly against anxiety about the future. An insurance salesman might claim that, with Jesus, he is seeking to eliminate anxiety, since adequate insurance coverage, in various areas, can free us from anxiety. But the method the insurance company uses and the method Jesus teaches us to use are not the same. Jesus taught that we can be free of anxiety by seeking first the Kingdom and being assured of the Father's provision. This is true even when we have not laid up treasures on earth and even if we have given away all that we possess. In other words, our financial resources may be minimal, but if we are approaching life properly, we can still be free from anxiety.

The insurance company solution involves becoming so strong economically that there is nothing to fear. This economic strength is achieved by making sure that we have the right relationship with an organization which has laid up such a vast amount of earthly treasure that it is impossible to imagine any situation which could overtax its resources. Again, I ask the question, isn't this precisely what Jesus said is unnecessary and unwise, the very thing he was speaking against?

Furthermore, if you look closely you will find that no economic solution to economic anxiety works. Once you take that route, there is no secure stopping place. You never have quite enough insurance. The only adequate solution to economic anxiety is a theological one. God alone is big enough and resourceful enough to enable us to survive all forseeable crises. Even the insurance companies, which look so big and strong, will be completely impotent if and when our whole economic system collapses. But God will always be there for us.

Insurance also involves putting sizable amounts of money aside to pay for future needs which may or may not arise, when I could be putting that same money into meeting needs of other people which are already a reality. We live in a world where millions are starving and many more are living in great poverty. Instead of making my resources available to meet their existing needs—if I take out insurance—I am choosing to put my money into meeting a future need of my own which may or may not materialize. Some events may seem pretty predictable, but let us not forget that the life of nations and cultures ebbs and flows like a "mist," as James says (4:14), and in ways that are often unpredictable and uncontrollable. We may pour a lot of money into preparing for future contingencies which will never come to pass. Like the farmer of Luke 12, we may prepare for early retirement but face sudden death. The contingency we envision may be the wrong one.

It is with this in mind that Jesus urges us to create "purses that do not grow old, . . . a treasure in the heavens" (Lk 12:33). The extra money we invest with God will serve us well in this life and in the age to come. We will be secure whether our economy survives or not. Doing it in the way Jesus suggests is the only way that we can be absolutely prepared for the future. And it has the added advantage of maximizing currently available resources to meet human need. I believe we need to seek alternative ways to deal with the same set of needs and problems which are addressed by the insurance companies. This could be a significant Christian ministry in our time. What would it look like?

First, any believer who is sincerely seeking first the Kingdom of God already has "complete coverage" for all his needs and liabilities. The protection he has is both more comprehensive and more secure than that offered by any of the big insurance companies. God himself has promised to be our protector and provider (Heb 13:5-6). If you qualify for the Kingdom benefits, the money you are putting into other policies represents double coverage. Our Fellowship has been relying on God to meet our needs for the past twenty-five years, and he has come through wonderfully.

If more of us stop taking out insurance, there will be more of us in situations where we need help from beyond ourselves. We would need to develop patterns of mutual aid within the Christian movement. This is good. We should do it. The Christian church has some very powerful economic muscles which aren't very well developed. It would be a great thing to see some of these potential capabilities developed through regular utilization.

In developing patterns of Christian mutual aid, I do not suggest that we simply create an insurance company which is owned and operated by Christians. That in itself might be valuable, but it would always tend to perpetuate some of the problematic features of the world's system. We should avoid creating an alternative which relys heavily upon accumulated financial reserves. It also seems to me we should look for ways of helping each other which are more congregational, instead of relating individuals to a central office. The point of a Christian alternative would be to discover that we can help each other, and that we can get along without large reserves if we are putting our trust in God and sharing freely.

The Amish are an interesting example of a brotherhood approach which does not rely upon an insurance company structure. The Amish have a strong commitment to help other members of their church whenever large and unusual needs arise. Most Amish groups carry no insurance, and they have also refused to get into the social security system. This protest has been upheld in court.

When sickness or an accident occurs, in the Amish context, the individual family is always expected to do as much as it can to meet the need. Maximum individual responsibility is maintained. There are no prearranged repayment schemes to blur this. But if the need goes beyond what the individual can reasonably bear, the local congregation assists them. And if the situation is too big for the local congregation, other congregations are asked to assist. The circle gets enlarged, as much as necessary, to meet whatever situation may arise.

The need is established in a consultation between the individual and several older and more mature brethren who know the situation well. The local deacon is responsible to see that this takes place. If a barn burns down, the brethren will usually gather on the following day to estimate the amount of the loss and determine what portion of this should be met by the church.

Once the amount of money needed has been established, it is divided among the family units present in whatever circle is being addressed with the need. The contribution of this assessed amount is still voluntary. Each individual and family must decide what they can do. The initial assessment simply determines that if all families involved contributed a certain amount, the need will be met. The deacon in each congregation then pays a personal visit to all of the families in the church to collect the money, and in the context of this personal visit, adjustments can be made. Families unable to contribute the suggested amount may be affirmed in their decision to give less, while families who are able to give more can likewise be encouraged to do so.

In this way all needs are adequately met. Even large amounts of money can be secured when necessary, by enlarging the circle. And no money is tied up in centralized reserves to cover potential contingencies. All current funds are available for current needs, yet through sharing, assistance is also available when it is needed. The whole process is kept local and congregational. Needs for assistance are defined by local persons who know the entire situation and are met in a manner that enhances a sense of local brotherhood. Since administration of economic assistance flows within established congregational structures, no time and money is needed to maintain an insurance office or organization. And there are, of course, no profits and no salaries. It is economically efficient and effective.

Of course, an alternative structure such as this would not in itself be significant apart from a strong faith in God and a spirit of love towards the brotherhood. With these, however, alternative economic forms can and should be considered.

In lifting up these questions about how Christians view insurance, I do not mean to obscure the complexity of the situations in which we are involved. For instance, through relationship to other persons and organizations we are often required to have insurance. Thus, even when our own choice would be to forgo the insurance, the choice is not altogether our own. In some situations, the state itself requires certain forms of insurance. Banks and businesses often require it as a precondition for certain relationships or transactions.

Of course, the choice is always our own. And a real purist might refuse, in all of these situations, to have anything to do with an insurance company. Our own approach, over the years, has been a more moderate one, participating when it was required of us by others, but choosing not to insure where it is primarily our own choice. It might seem, on first thought, that there are so many areas in which insurance is required, that this leaves very little to our own personal choice. But this is not really the case. And I think any Christian looking for other alternatives will be surprised at the number of places in which alternatives are possible.

A much more profound question concerns the practical impact of having or not having insurance. Would not a Christian community which took the path of avoiding insurance find itself gravely burdened with the responsibility of caring for a large number of retired, widowed, and disabled members? Isn't the small amount of money invested in insurance easily worth it in terms of the large financial burdens which are thereby avoided?

This is an unanswerable question—apart from accumulated experience. Thus far, our twenty-five years of following an alternative approach have worked amazingly well. And my faith is that God will enable his people to adequately care for the needy without becoming overwhelmed in the process. But the risks are great. And even at best, the task of caring for the aged and disabled will always be a significant one, rightly claiming a significant portion of our resources.

In the total picture, it seems obvious that using insurance tends to increase the cost of caring for these needs. Besides large profits going to the insurance industry, the cost of settlements tends to increase because of the vast, almost unlimited resources of insurance companies. In all areas covered by insurance, the persons who suffer loss as well as those who are helping them to repair or overcome the loss, tend to raise their sights considerably because of the large insurance company resources. The vast amounts of money tend to excite greed, which lies close at hand for us all. In the total picture, insurance is not the cheapest way to deal with these needs.

Nor is it always the best. Because insurance is almost the universal solution to mutual aid problems, families and churches tend to minimize their own commitment to help. Thus when adequate insurance coverage is not available, the person in need may suffer with very little assistance being offered. And because insurance coverage is determined by prearranged contract, some elements of the need are frequently neglected in the pattern of settlement.

Devising a practical alternative to the present insurance system is certainly a difficult and costly path. How well such alternatives will work remains to be seen. The ultimate justification for an alternative approach is not, however, on a practical level, but on a theological one. Sound theology should bring good practical results. But a strictly pragmatic analysis does not necessarily lead to sound theological conclusions.

Many Christians do not find enough theological question in this realm of insurance to warrant any new thoughts and actions. But a significant number of Christians are becoming concerned about these, issues. To these especially, I commend these reflections.

Missionary Strategy

A fuller grasp of the economic principles of the Kingdom of God could greatly enhance the world missionary capabilities of the Christian movement. First, a good application of these scriptural principles will help free people for mission and adequately prepare them. Too much devotion to the economic pursuits of life deters Christians throughout the world from their great missionary task. If the normal expectation for all believers was a thorough renunciation of these claims, a greater concentration of energy could go into advancing the Christian witness throughout the world.

Furthermore, a more active pattern of giving and sharing

within the local Christian brotherhood provides good training in personal maturity and in the exercise of spiritual gifts which are vital to any larger missionary assignment. As we try to make our faith practical by ministering to one another, we will discover limitations within ourselves which we didn't know existed. We also learn greater sensitivity and humility in serving others. Experience with such ministry, in modest everyday situations within our own culture, helps develop gifts which will be useful in trans-cultural ministry. Too many missionary candidates have been sent out to perform a level of ministry in a strange culture which far exceeds anything they have attempted in their own, and the normal process of growth in ministry gets mixed with the process of cultural translation. Under these circumstances it is difficult to identify the limitations which originate with our own pride and unexamined cultural assumptions. Since so many of the world's peoples struggle with questions of poverty and economics, we would do well to deal with these issues in our own culture, with Christian brothers and sisters. In doing this, we would also gain valuable insights into the relationship between "church" and "world" which is always a strategic issue in missionary situations. We need to grapple more seriously with the limitations of culture and the costliness of following Christ, while discovering the value of cultural forms and the necessity of finding appropriate Christian adaptations. Trans-cultural missionaries who are over-dependent upon their own culture often expect too much or too little from their "foreign" converts and colleagues. Working with the economic principles of the Kingdom of God helps us to gain perspective on ourselves as well as on the culture in which we live. And the more we can help one another to zealously seek first the Kingdom of God, the more we can create an environment in which people can hear God calling them to special assignments and ministry in other parts of the world.

A second way in which a fuller application of Kingdom principles in our economic life could enhance the missionary capabilities of the church would be the increase of funds and resources available for world mission. If more Christians could catch the vision of laying up treasures in heaven, a great deal of money currently located in savings accounts, insurance policies, and other forms of accumulated assets could be rechanneled into world mission. This would certainly be an opportune time in world history for a great outpouring of Christian resources for all sorts of mission. Besides the release of accumulated capital, a fuller grasp of Kingdom principles would allow many believers to freely share a greater portion of their current earnings.

A third sphere of application concerns the potential for sending out apostolic companies. When Jesus sent out his twelve disciples to preach the Gospel of the Kingdom and heal the sick (Mt 10), he restated some of his general understanding of Kingdom economics and applied them to the sending out of an apostolic team. He said, "You received without paying, give without pay. Take no gold, nor silver, nor copper in your belts, no bag for your journey, nor two tunics, nor sandals, nor a staff; for the laborer deserves his food" (Mt 10:8-10).

This was not an approach limited strictly to the Twelve. Jesus gave a similar instruction to the seventy disciples when they were sent out two by two: "Carry no purse, no bag, no sandals; and salute no one on the road. Whatever house you enter, first say, 'Peace be to this house!' And if a son of peace is there, your peace shall rest upon him; but if not, it shall return to you. And remain in the same house, eating and drinking what they provide, for the laborer deserves his wages; do not go from house to house" (Lk 10:4-7).

These principles of missionary economics need much more exploration and application in our own time. What are the main points? First, Jesus sent his missionary companies out with no money and with no prospect of receiving support from the sending base. We are so accustomed to supporting missionaries with money from home that this is astounding! How could we send them without money? Yet Jesus was completely confident that the Father would take care of them, just as he said in his teaching! He even specifies that the missionary can expect to find food and lodging among those to whom he preaches. And if such a local welcome is withheld, Jesus tells the disciples to move on. Time is short, and they need to concentrate where people are open to the message.

The expectation that the laborer deserves his wages could lead to misunderstanding. But, as recorded in Matthew, Jesus prefaced his instructions with "You received without paying, give without pay" (Mt 10:8). Matthew also uses the word "food" instead of "wages." In other words, there should be no thought of personal gain among those who go out on mission. The missionary has a priceless treasure to share—a message of God's love, power and healing. Let this not be contaminated or diminished by seeking personal benefits for ourselves. Yet the laborer deserves food and sustenance, the necessities of life. These will be provided.

Jesus, then, advocates sending such traveling apostolic groups out with no financial reserves, to give themselves to preaching the Gospel. If they are content to receive simple food and lodging, they will, in fact, be furnished with all that they need by the people to whom they go. Jesus queried the disciples later on, "When I sent you out with no purse or bag or sandals, did you lack anything?" and they said, "Nothing" (Lk 22:35). A similar testimony can be shared by others who have followed the same approach. It works.

By sending missionaries out in this way, Jesus bypassed some of the problems which have been most difficult in the history of Christian missions. Because the apostles came with nothing and were hosted by local persons, they didn't create a separate sphere of experience which represented a transplant of their own hometown culture. They brought very little except the message itself. Their stay was temporary, and the whole development was indigenous from the very beginning. Furthermore, because the preaching of the Gospel required local hospitality, Jesus' approach facilitated rapid development of relationships with local persons. It also gave some responsibility to them; they were on the giving end, as well as the receiving end, of the process, right from the beginning. Some local family was assuming responsibility for the mission.

Paul seems to have followed a similar pattern in his own missionary travels, concentrating on short-term efforts in a variety of places and trusting God to make the missionary team a financially self-sustaining effort. We see in his experience some variations on the theme. In some situations he specifically refrained from receiving support from local people because he wanted to make the Gospel even more "free" (1 Cor 9:18) and to expose those who were abusing the apostolic privilege (2 Cor 11:12). To achieve this, he supported himself with tent-making (Acts 20:34) and with aid received from other churches (2 Cor 11:8).

The potential for traveling, self-supporting, apostolic-type groups still exists and warrants greater attention. Such groups can still go out in the confidence that "the Lord commanded that those who proclaim the gospel should get their living by the gospel" (1 Cor 9:14). This principle may have an application in the settled ministry of congregational leaders, but the particular focus for Jesus and for Paul was an apostolic, missionary one. We can go forth without money and expect to be supported.

Of course, the fact that this potential exists doesn't mean we should always do it that way. We have already noted that Paul did not always receive support from the town in which he was ministering. He did accept support from other churches. Other kinds of support arrangements are particularly relevant when the missionary group intends to settle down for a longer period. But when we settle in for long periods, especially in trans-cultural mission, we need to be highly sensitive to the dangers of cultural imperialism and gospel/culture confusions.

Yet even under these circumstances, which might be described as trans-cultural migration for the sake of mission, going in with less money would often be helpful. Trusting more and bringing less could have minimized some of the difficulties of trans-cultural mission. The more we bring with us, the more we tend to separate ourselves from the local situation. On the other hand, the more fully we can share the life and culture of the people to whom we minister—eating their food, as Jesus recommended—the more we can open channels of relationships for sharing the Good News.

A fuller application of Kingdom economic principles will undergird world mission in yet another way. When we discover how much our daily life, even our daily bread, is to be received by faith, and we learn how to look to God and ask him for all that we need, we will grow in our capacity to live by faith. A faith approach to life is vital to mission. In mission efforts, projects must often be launched on the basis of vision. We must move forward simply because we hear the Lord calling us to move forward. Responsibilities must often be undertaken without knowing where all the money will come from. Learning to trust our Father in heaven and to receive from him all that we need as we do his will is a lesson crucial to a strong missionary thrust, and working out some of these steps in our economic life as individuals and local churches is a way to integrate this lesson in a realistic, down-to-earth fashion.

Covenant Economics

"Do good unto all men but especially to those who are of the household of faith" (Gal 6:10). To understand the practice of the early church we must pay attention to the unique covenant relationship that exists among Christian believers. Christian charity extends to all persons, but has a special significance within the household of faith. If we want to implement the economic teachings of Jesus, we must recover a more lively sense of the church as a covenant brotherhood, one with economic implications.

This is inferred at a number of points in the New Testament. At Jerusalem, "there was not a needy person *among them*" (Acts 4:34). While these early believers must certainly have served and aided many other poor persons who were living in Jerusalem, it was particularly among the believers—who shared a covenant relationship—that there was a level of sharing and a commitment to see that all needs were met. When this sharing process started breaking down and one sector of the Christian community was not getting adequate care (Acts 6:1), administrative changes were made to correct the problem. The community of faith was committed to maintaining this level of sharing.

The two parts of this covenant relationship are illustrated in the experience of Jesus with his twelve disciples. Among themselves they operated with a common fund, of which Judas was the administrator (Jn 13:29), and from this fund they distributed alms to the poor. They did not distribute alms to one another, but shared in a more systematic, organized way. Nor did they seek to enter into a common fund relationship with others outside the circle of disciples.

So the covenant relationship between brothers and sisters in the Christian church defined a unique level of economic responsibility for one another. When there was famine in the land, the believers in Antioch sent aid to the "brethren" in Judea (Acts 11:29). The strong words of the Apostle John have the same focus: "If any one has this world's goods and sees his *brother* in need, yet closes his heart . . . " (1 Jn 3:17).

It is quite possible that the famous Parable of the Last Judgment, as recorded in Matthew 25, actually focuses especially on our responsibility to fellow believers." "As you did it to one of the least of these *my brethren*, you did it to me" (Mt 25:40). In the New Testament, the term "brethren" often specifically means "fellow believers." Jesus uses the term this way in some of this teachings: "If your *brother* sins . . . " (Mt 18:15). And elsewhere he is very explicit about the unique significance of charity extended to someone because they are disciples. "Whoever gives to one of these little ones even a cup of cold water, *because he is a disciple*, truly I say to you, he shall not lose his reward" (Mt 10:42). The parallelism between Matthew 10 and Matthew 25 is striking. In both passages Jesus is pointing his hearers towards the ultimate "reward." Those receiving assistance are characterized as "little ones" or "one of the least." In Matthew 10, the recipients are designated "disciples," in Matthew 25, "brethren."

If Matthew 25 is, in fact, a strong call for mutual aid among Christian brethren, there are still, of course, many other teachings in the Gospel regarding our duty to serve all men and to bind up the wounds of any neighbor, regardless of his faith. We are called to love even our enemies. We must do both, but the difference is important. Our relationship to the enemy whom we love differs from our relationship to the brother whom we love. We are charged to "do good unto all men, but especially to those who are of the household of faith."

When Paul spoke of equality and used the analogy of Israel in the wilderness, he was clearly envisioning a pattern of redistribution among "the brethren." The level of expectation and implementation differs greatly as between what is possible on the broader world scene. The church is our proving ground, the place where we should make it work. Then out of the uniqueness of what God has done within the church, our love and generosity will overflow into the world at large. If we can learn how to conduct Kingdom economics "among ourselves," we will have a context in which to extend the same principles to others. Sometimes it seems that we Christians feel so guilty for having done so little for the world that we try to compensate by doing too much. In our shame, we neglect to take the time and resources to see that the brethern are properly cared for, and we want immediately to universalize all of our efforts and make an impact upon the whole world. If I may paraphrase a line from 1 Peter, "The time has come for charity to begin with the household of God, and if it begins with us, where will it end?"

SIX

God Fulfills His Promises

THESE KINGDOM OF GOD economic principles, which are presented in Scripture, should be viewed primarily as life-giving promises, rather than as burdensome and unwelcome restrictions. It is through these "precious and very great promises," as Peter observed (2 Pt 1:4), "that we are able to escape the corruption that is in the world because of passion, and become partakers of the divine nature." Peter, of course, was referring to all the promises of God, not the economic ones in particular. But this perspective on the situation applies well to the economic aspects of the Gospel.

God has extended himself to us in terms of precious and very great promises. Many of these are specifically economic in nature. Why can't we move much more boldly to guild an economic strategy based upon the promises of God? In financial matters, so much depends upon promises. Workers give their labor on the strength of promises. Investments, sales, and loans of all sorts are extended on the basis of promises. Trust in promises is the basis for economic movement and growth. God has pledged himself to us in economic promises. We can move on them with confidence.

I would like to give testimony to the faithfulness of God in fulfilling his economic promises. Reba Place Fellowship will celebrate its 25th anniversary this year. From the very beginning we were inspired by the teachings of Jesus in the area of economics. We wanted to put these things into practice and prove his word. This led us to take a number of unusual steps. People who had assets sold them and gave the proceeds to charity. Or, as in the early church, many of them brought all of their resources and gave them to the church for redistribution. This kind of "Jubilee" release has occurred again and again throughout the years. Many sizeable inheritances have been redistributed to serve the Kingdom of God.

We have encouraged one another to be content with a moderate standard of living, to avoid accumulation, to avoid insurance, to avoid indebtedness. Loans have been made without interest. Outstanding debts have been cancelled without repayment. Grants and gifts of various sorts have been extended to many persons in need.

Within the Fellowship, God has graciously helped us to supply everyone's need, so that it can truly be said there has not been a needy person among us. Yet our doors have been open to all sorts of people, and many needy persons have come to us and become part of our life. God has given extra resources to care for the extra people. And through a system of sharing those who gathered little have had no lack. A general level of equality has been sustained among all the members. For most of the members, over most of these years, this has been achieved by sharing all that we have in a common treasury.

The greatest deterrent toward measures of this sort is the fear that it will not work. We wonder whether our needs will be met, or whether we will be able to function adequately in our society. And what about the future? This is the point to which I am speaking. God has faithfully and abundantly supplied our needs, fulfilling his promises, over a period of many years.

Even though we gave away many of our possessions and let go of other "normal" economic strategies, we have had plenty. God himself has supplied our need. We have given generously, we have received generously. We have let go of economic resources, but God has supplied economic resources as they have been needed. There is a remarkable correlation in our life between unusual needs and unusual resources.

We tend to operate on a close budget, without much accumulation toward future goals or unexpected needs. We use and share what God gives, and trust that he will provide for us as we go along. Because of God's faithfulness, wonderful things have happened to us in the process. Our immediate needs have been met, and we have also been able to share with others, as well as to care for large and unexpected situations as they have arisen. We have often been protected from accidents and illness. But when these have occurred, we have experienced the supply of God's resources to cover our expenses.

Besides meeting our immediate needs, God has wonderfully enabled us to secure housing in one particular neighborhood so that we can live close to one another and share a life of Christian community. Even though housing in Evanston is scarce, and quite costly, as the Fellowship has grown we have been able to secure housing when it was needed. Without seeking to accumulate the capital necessary to do so, we have in fact, been able to purchase a number of homes and apartment buildings.

When we needed a larger meeting place, a suitable building in our immediate neighborhood became available in what seemed to be an obviously providential manner. Furthermore, without our having planned for it, the money for purchase of the building also became available at the same time. The building—once an old garage—needed extensive repair and remodeling before it would be useable for meetings. So for a whole year, a sizeable crew was at work on the building. God enabled us to support the crew and pay for the materials. So, in a period of about fourteen months we came up with an extra $300,000, without any unusual fund raising or special economic strategies. We had a need, and God wonderously supplied the need.

We have often added someone to our full-time staff when the budget was already stretched to the limit, just because it seemed that God was leading us to do so. And by his grace, things have worked out and we have been able to meet our expenses. We have frequently had big contributors move away, and needy people move in—yet God continues to help us balance the budget.

I am sure there is much we can learn about managing our finances well, about making greater sacrifices, and about investing more wisely for the Kingdom of God. But insofar as we have put Kingdom of God principles into action, we have found God's faithful protection and abundant supply to be our constant response.

We have also experienced the personal, spiritual, and social advantages of which Jesus spoke. Many of our people have been amazingly free of economic anxiety—at a time when anxiety runs high in the broader society—and they have experienced considerable freedom to seek first the Kingdom of God.

Our application of these Kingdom principles has been very imperfect. I want to make that clear. But God's response has been unmistakable and wonderful. What Paul affirmed has been illustrated in our experience time and again:

> He who sows sparingly will also reap sparingly, and he who sows bountifully will also reap bountifully. . . . God is able to provide you with every blessing in abundance, so that you may always have enough of everything and may provide in abudance for every good work. (2 Cor 9:6-8)

For Such a Time as This

To wealthy and prosperous Christians who may read this book, I conclude with the following question, "Is it possible that you have come to the Kingdom for such a time as this?"

Uncle Mordecai first put this question to Queen Esther, inviting her to utilize her position of power and privilege in an effort to save her people from extinction (Est 4:14). Esther was in a strategic position. Yet it was not certain that she could, in fact, accomplish anything for her people. If she tried and failed, she would lose her own life. But if her mission succeeded, her people would be saved. Esther's courageous choice, and the successful outcome of her saving intervention, have made this a favorite Bible story for many generations.

The story gives us a useful analogy for "Rich Christians in an Age of Hunger," as Ron Sider has aptly labelled us. Is it possible that we have come to this place of power and privilege for just such a time?

Some have wondered, what was a nice Jewish girl doing as queen to King Ahasuerus in Susa? Does not her presence in the palace already represent a significant compromise of faith and of Jewish identity? Perhaps. But that was obviously an irrelevant question as the crisis of her time unfolded. Mordecai wasted no time on whether she should have been there. He was totally focused on what she should do, given the fact that she was the queen.

In similar fashion, many people in our time have wondered what all those nice Christians are doing in the present-day centers of wealth and power. Doesn't this already represent a significant compromise of faith and Christian identity? Perhaps. But again, the crucial question is what are we going to do, now that we are here? Is it possible that you—and I—have come to the Kingdom for just such a time?

For us, as for Esther, the call to action involves the question of personal survival, as well as serving the welfare of others. "Think not," warned Mordecai, "that in the king's palace you will escape any more than all the other Jews" (Est 4:13). Wealthy Christians need a bold application of Kingdom of God economic principles for the sake of their own survival. In our highly developed technological society the power of mammon becomes ever more effective in its control over the life of persons and organizations. Without clear and deliberate alternative strategies, Christian people and Christian organizations get co-opted by the world. Without needing to give up their explicit profession of faith, they are rendered increasingly impotent in the exercise of this faith. Thus, even though we might wonder, as did Esther, whether we can survive if we do step out boldly in faith, it becomes increasingly clear that we shall not survive if we fail to act.

However, it is not simply for our own survival that wealthy Christians are called to new steps of faith others are waiting to

Christians are callied to new steps of faith others are waiting to be saved. The lives of many people hang in the balances. Multitudes are threatened with extinction. This is true in spiritual terms—how many people all over the world are dying without any knowledge of the Kingdom of God and the salvation which comes through Jesus Christ? It is also true in a physical sense; because of war and famine, many millions are perishing for lack of daily food and the bare necessities of life. Is it possible that you are called to risk your life and your resources, so that others may be saved, and so that you may truly "find" your own life? What could happen if all of your resources were totally mobilized for the Kingdom of God?

We should not be naive as we venture forth in response to the call of God. Confronting world mission and world poverty is a very complex and exceedingly difficult task. Much more is required than the simple investment of funds and human energies, for we are not wrestling against flesh and blood, but against spiritual powers and principalities. The proper investment of our resources and energies is important, and the zealous exercise of our spiritual resources is absolutely critical. It is time for a total effort.

When we look at the world from a spiritual perspective, we get to the same question even more urgently—is it possible that you have come to the Kingdom for such a time as this?

This is the day the Lord has given us. Let us withhold nothing. The time for a total mobilization of Christian resources for world mission is at hand.

www.ingramcontent.com/pod-product-compliance
Lightning Source LLC
LaVergne TN
LVHW020643100826
845148LV00012B/2313